Fruitful

BECOMING WHO GOD CREATED YOU TO BE

D1444845

ERIC MICHAEL BRYANT

Fruitful: Becoming Who God Created You To Be by Eric Michael Bryant

Published by Catalyzing Community
3600 Denbar Court
Austin, TX 78739

www.ericbryant.org

Cover and Interior by Benjamin Sledge | https://benjaminsledge.com

Some of this material was shared at Mosaic in Los Angeles from 2002 to 2010 and at Gateway Church in Austin from 2013 to 2021.

ISBN: 978-1-7375646-0-7

Printed in United States of America

First edition

To Caleb and Trevi, I am so grateful God entrusted you to us. I am so proud of who you are.

To our extended family, our Mosaic church family, our Gateway church family, our friends and neighbors in Los Angeles and South Austin, thank you for investing in our children and helping them along in their journey.

To Deborah, I am so grateful to be your partner in this adventure.

To Jesus, you are our Rescuer, our Way, our Truth, and our Life.

CONTENTS

For *Fruitful*

"Eric Michael Bryant has done it again! The conversation he advances in **Fruitful** *is not only timely but invaluable for this next generation. Eric shares personal insights and truths from the Scriptures in ways that will inspire you, challenge you, and cause you to consider where you are in your walk with God and in relations to others."*

- Marcus "Goodie" Goodloe, Ph.D., Author, Martin Luther King Jr. Scholar, and Leadership Development Consultant

"Eric Bryant humbly and simply shares his thoughtful reflections on how to live a life of faith, hope and love."

- Dave Gibbons, Founder of NEWSONG CHURCH and Author of Small Cloud Rising

For *Not Like Me*

"Not Like Me is all about the heart and the how of evangelism. Bryant's style and substance reflect a refreshing departure from ineffective, shame-based witnessing techniques...and a return to the simple and compelling compassion of Christ."

- Steven Furtick, Lead Pastor, Elevation Church, Charlotte, NC

"Authors ought to write with authenticity and books ought to be enjoyable to read. This book is both. Eric Bryant is the real deal. And Not Like Me will challenge the way you think while putting a smile on your face!"

- Mark Batterson, lead pastor of National Community Church in

Washington, D.C. and author of Whisper and Circle Maker

"Winsome, honest, theologically grounded – Bryant's work calls us to move beyond the theory of bridge building to everyday, practical choices for actually loving others as Jesus loved."

- Nancy Beach, Willow Creek Association

"Not Like Me gets to the heart of our emotions to invoke in us the desire to be more like Jesus; to reach out to others, to face our own selfishness and be about Jesus' mission. Thanks, Eric, for this challenging book!

- Dave Ferguson, Lead Pastor, Community Christian Church Chicago, IL and author of B.L.E.S.S.

"Not Like Me is a brilliant field guide to help leaders and all Christ-followers understand how to engage with and influence a diverse world. Eric tackles the topics of diversity that frighten most Christians and cause them to withdraw from the world around them. With a firm grounding in Scripture, Eric helps us know how to bring light into the darkness rather than just curse the darkness. Not Like Me helps us understand the positive side of difference which we need to truly understand the Creator."

- John Burke, Senior Pastor, Gateway Church in Austin and author of Imagine Heaven

"Eric knows what he's talking about, and he practices what he preaches. Not Like Me is Saving Private Ryan meets Nacho Libre! Eric calls us to a heroic mission and at the same time exposes our flawed humanity. He tackles one of the most critical and complex issues of our time and brings it down to earth and keeps us grounded in reality. It's quite a gift to force us to face such uncomfortable and serious issues and at the same time to keep us laughing."

- Erwin McManus, Lead Pastor at Mosaic in Los Angeles, Author of The Genius of Jesus

AN INTRODUCTION

"Dad, before I go, I want you to write down all you wish you knew before you left your parents' house."

My daughter Trevi knows what she wants and usually knows how to get it, but this time I was her obstacle.

The thought of her leaving the house after high school stopped me in my tracks.

I knew it was inevitable. My wife and I had been preparing for this for a long time. Still—was it already time?

It was hard to move forward because I had so much to say. Where to even start?

I had already said so much.

There is so much I don't know about the future anymore.

As part of the class of 2020, Trevi's senior year did not end quite like she hoped, or anyone expected. She made the best of it, and even created some really fun memories. Prophetically, on the Thursday before Senior Skip Day, which comes just before spring break, she jokingly told everyone goodbye in case they didn't come back after spring break.

In Austin where we live, the massive city-wide conference South by Southwest (SXSW) had been cancelled, but up to that point we had not expected school to move online for the rest of the semester. So no prom. No graduation. Even the school day the seniors were supposed to skip was cancelled.

What we have experienced since the spring of 2020 has been unprecedented.

- A highly contagious pandemic, which has killed far too many people. Economically, many more were devastated—losing a job or losing their business.
- In addition, the pandemic revealed the glaring racial disparities in our world. The protests and the riots after the death of George Floyd reignited a cultural conversation on racial justice, white supremacy, and systemic racism. This continued with rallies to #StopAsianHate in 2021, as hate crimes have been on the rise.
- The political division in the United States bubbled over onto social media with people being divided on almost every topic. This has continued well after the contentious 2020 election.

With all the uncertainty and chaos going on in our world, I still have hope. I have seen the resilience of my children, who are now young adults. I have seen their generation willing to join the conversation and bring about genuine and lasting change in our world.

For my children, my nieces and nephews along with my cousins and their children, and for those growing up in a world shaped by 9/11, the Great Recession, school shootings, and now a pandemic and a movement against systemic racism, my hope for you is that you will become the person God created you to be.

Our world *needs* you to become the person God created you to be.

- Our world needs more young women and young

men who discover the genuine faith, love, and hope God brings through an authentic relationship with Jesus. Unfortunately, American religiosity and churchianity has created hypocrisy, judgmentalism, nationalism, and division.

- Our world needs more young women and young men to not only pray the Lord's prayer but to truly bring about God's kingdom on earth as it is in heaven. Unfortunately, too often the church has attempted to be a refuge *from* the world rather than a refuge *for* the world.
- Our world needs you.

Jesus told a parable that has been a guide for me over the years and which I think summarizes well my hope for you.

The parable of the soils describes four different types of people: Those who never connect to faith because they never respond to God's Word; those whose faith disappears when things get tough; those who get distracted from their faith; and those who fulfill their potential and become fruitful.

If you can develop the four characteristics inspired by the parable of the four soils, you will discover your calling and bring about so much good in our broken world.

The first three characteristics describe the antidote to the first three soils, and the fourth characteristic describes the fourth soil.

You can learn how to become RECEPTIVE by knowing God personally and discerning how to hear His voice rather than not responding to the Word of God.

You can learn how to become TENACIOUS by trusting the Scriptures and living out your God-given identity, rather than giving up when facing the time of testing.

You can learn how to become INTENTIONAL by making wise choices and ending the cycle of brokenness in our families rather than being choked by life's worries, riches, and pleasures.

You can learn how to become PROACTIVE by loving, serving, and reaching others.

A spiritually receptive, tenacious, intentional, and proactive person will experience the presence and peace of God and have one hundred times the impact.

That is my hope for you.

THE FRUITFUL LIFE

That same day Jesus went out of the house and sat by the lake. Such large crowds gathered around him that he got into a boat and sat in it, while all the people stood on the shore. Then he told them many things in parables, saying:

"A farmer went out to sow his seed. As he was scattering the seed, some fell along the path, and the birds came and ate it up. Some fell on rocky places, where it did not have much soil. It sprang up quickly, because the soil was shallow. But when the sun came up, the plants were scorched, and they withered because they had no root. Other seed fell among thorns, which grew up and choked the plants. Still other seed fell on good soil, where it produced a crop—a hundred, sixty or thirty times what was sown. Whoever has ears, let them hear."

"Listen then to what the parable of the sower means: When anyone hears the message about the kingdom and does not understand it, the evil one comes and snatches away what was sown in their heart. This is the seed sown along the path. The seed falling on rocky ground refers to someone who hears the word and at once receives it with joy. But since they have no root, they last only a short time. When trouble or persecution comes because of the word, they quickly fall away. The seed falling among the thorns refers to someone who hears the word, but the worries of this life and the deceitfulness of wealth choke the word, making it unfruitful. But the seed falling on good soil refers to someone who hears the word and understands it. This is the one who produces a crop, yielding a hundred, sixty or thirty times what was sown." (Matthew 13:1-9, 18-23, NIV)

OF ALL THE messages Jesus could share in front of one of the biggest crowds ever gathered around Him, you might be surprised He chose this specific message. He didn't start this message from the boat talking about life after death. He didn't talk about wealth or poverty. Instead, Jesus described a journey toward becoming fruitful.

Jesus tells us that in His kingdom you have unlimited potential.

God has greater ideas in mind for our lives than we do. Our fears, weaknesses, past mistakes, regrets, and background cannot prevent us from experiencing God and impacting others in dramatic ways.

Jesus is sharing about the invisible kingdom of God—a kingdom that will one day include people from every nation, a kingdom that advances with peace, love, faith, and hope, rather than through war and destruction. Jesus is the King of a new kingdom that does not separate people by establishing borders, but rather eliminates borders and includes all who desire to let Him be their King.

We can experience a life beyond our wildest imagination when we maximize who we were created to be. Applying the principles Jesus shared in describing the four types of soils, we can become fruitful (a.k.a., creative, generative, and productive) for the kingdom of God. Jesus' parable points out that we struggle to become who we were created to be when we have a hardened heart, a shallow faith, or find ourselves trapped among the thorns. If we can avoid these pitfalls, we will be fruitful.

Which soil do you think best describes where you are in your spiritual journey?

1. The Rocky Path: A hardened heart
2. The Shallow Soil: A shallow faith
3. The Path with Thorns: A distracted person
4. The Rich and Fertile Soil: The fruitful life

Another way to look at this would be to consider which of these categories best describes your most common approach to faith:

1. The Unreceptive: Those unwilling or unable to hear from God
2. The Quitters: Those easily discouraged by trials
3. The Distracted: Those easily derailed by temptations
4. The Fruitful: Those who are being transformed and transforming others

To avoid these common struggles, we can discover our God-given destiny by developing four characteristics. In my thirty years of ministry, I have seen people who are representative of each of the soils. I know people with outstanding potential who were not interested, quit when things got tough, or became distracted by things of this world. Understanding the urgency and importance of this journey, we can become who we were created to be, which means we need to become receptive, tenacious, intentional, and proactive.

An Identity Crisis

In our culture we seem to have an identity crisis. We lack clarity and purpose! Have you noticed this?

We have an intrinsic desire that drives us toward progress. We desire to become someone who matters. We long for purpose and meaning in life. A relationship with God brings guidance and clarity to our calling.

A couple years ago, my wife, Deborah, and I hosted a small group in our house near downtown Austin. We had some amazing people in our group. In the beginning, I encouraged everyone to pray and come up with spiritual goals they hoped to accomplish, which we then emailed to ourselves three months later through www.futureme.org.

FutureMe.org allows you to email yourself at a certain date in the future. It is quite mind-trippy to receive an email from your younger self! Three months later, most of us had forgotten we had even gone through this exercise, but a filmmaker in our group named Scott brought his email. He printed it out, because he was so excited about all that had come to pass during our group. With genuine excitement Scott showed us how everything on his list had happened, plus amazing things he hadn't even considered!

At the peak of his excitement, a friend of ours in the group said, "Well, nothing on my list happened." Unsure of how to respond in that moment, we all sat in silence. Momentum had been lost, until she said one of the most insightful things ever shared in our group. She then said, "The difference is that you worked hard to make so much progress, and I didn't work at it at all."

Here's the truth: **God works in our lives and even helps us trust Him, but there are things we must do to really grow.** We have to work hard to overcome a hardened heart, trials, temptations, and selfishness. We need to choose to follow Him, which is not always easy.

What Does It Mean to Be Fruitful?

We will look at how developing these new characteristics in our life can help us make progress in our spiritual journey.

These character traits are derived from Jesus' parable of the soils. To avoid being like the rocky soil, we must overcome a hard heart by becoming receptive to God's voice. To move from a shallow faith to a deep faith, we must overcome trials by becoming tenacious. To move from a thorny situation and instead have clarity, we must overcome temptations by becoming intentional. To avoid a life of desolation, a life lacking fruitfulness, we must overcome selfishness by becoming proactive.

This chart shows us a way to apply the parable of the soils to our lives:

SOILS	WHAT CHANGES	CHARACTERISTICS
Hardened	A Soft Heart	*Receptive (Overcoming a Hard Heart)*
Shallow	A Deep Faith	*Tenacious (Overcoming Trials)*
Distracted	A Clear Plan	*Intentional (Overcoming Temptations)*
Desolate	A Fruitful Life	*Proactive (Overcoming Selfishness)*

Throughout the Scriptures, those who have a relationship with God through Jesus are challenged to bear fruit. Jesus and Paul talk about bearing fruit repeatedly. So, what does this mean?

In essence, "bearing fruit" is an expression that describes

changes in our lives or changes in the lives of others. These positive changes are the results of intentional decisions we make that shape how we live our lives. Our beliefs begin to shape how we live our lives. How we live our lives can influence what others believe.

Personal Transformation

Bearing fruit means a positive change in our own lives. Paul writes to the followers of Jesus in the city of Galatia to encourage them to live different lives now that they are following Him. He describes two types of people: those who live influenced by darkness which is the sinful nature and those who live by the Spirit.

He writes:

> The acts of the sinful nature are obvious: sexual immorality, impurity and debauchery; idolatry and witchcraft; hatred, discord, jealousy, fits of rage, selfish ambition, dissensions, factions and envy; drunkenness, orgies, and the like. I warn you, as I did before, that those who live like this will not inherit the kingdom of God. But the fruit of the Spirit is love, joy, peace, patience, kindness, goodness, faithfulness, gentleness and self-control. Against such things there is no law. (Galatians 5:19-23, NIV)

In a similar letter to the Corinthians, after the list of actions of someone stuck in the sinful nature, Paul adds the phrase: "And that is what some of you were" (1 Corinthians 6:11). This means that the church is made up of people who have been living this way, but the beauty is that we do not have to live that way anymore. We do not have to clean up our lives to get to God. Instead, we repent. We turn our lives over to God, asking Him to guide us in His ways and to change us out of gratitude for all He has done for us.

Our lives begin to be transformed when we no longer treat ourselves as the leader of our lives and let God lead us. People who know us should notice the difference in how we live our lives. Whether our life story is so dramatic that it should be a made-for-TV movie, or we have managed to live a sheltered life, our life should be different than it was before we chose to follow Jesus.

When we were part of Mosaic, a church in Los Angeles, one of the services met at a nightclub downtown. We had the opportunity to interact with many spiritual seekers over the years, who were willing to come to church in a nightclub but would never step foot in a church building. On one summer night several years ago, a friend of ours shared her spiritual story. She began her story by reading Galatians 5:17-21, the first part of the passage above. After reading the passage, she said, "Before I chose to follow Christ, I used to do all of these things." She stopped for a moment and then said, "Well, except for the orgies." It was way more information than we wanted to know, but she made her point. She was dramatically different now than she was before personally encountering God. By following Jesus, her life began to bear fruit. She was more righteous and more in step with the fruit of the Spirit.

Other passages refer to the "fruit of righteousness" (Philippians 1:11). We are to bear the "fruit of righteousness" because we have received the "fruit of the Spirit."

When we choose to turn from our sins toward following Jesus as our leader, we should become different people. We are no longer the same. "The old has gone the new has come" (2 Corinthians 5:17). People should notice that we are not as impatient, irritable, insecure, proud, immoral, and so on. The change takes place instantly as well as over time. God's Spirit within us convicts us and guides us.

Sadly, too many people have done a great deal of damage in the name of Jesus or even Christianity. Without exhibiting these beautiful traits of kindness, gentleness, love, and patience, religious Christians have imposed their view of the world on others who are not yet sure about faith. Their form of cultural Christianity has kept people from even exploring faith, because they spew condemnation, which comes from a place of darkness.

Too often we have allowed distorted versions of Christianity that have more in common with nationalism or Marxism than the teachings of Jesus to affect how we trust God and trust others. We have allowed others to steal from us what God wants to give us. We should not give the worst people in our lives so much power! Do not let the evil choices of others keep you from discovering the God who loves you and invites you into a life of purpose and meaning.

You see, a true follower of Jesus becomes more like Jesus.

With God's help, we can develop new patterns or habits in our lives. This life transformation often frustrates yet intrigues those who are closest to us. When we are being transformed by God, we may find that our family or friends who do not yet follow God resist these changes. They knew what to expect from us. Now they don't. We may even face persecution because those closest to us miss "the way we were" or because they feel compelled to consider the way they are living their own lives.

When our lives bear the fruit of righteousness and reflect the fruit of the Spirit, we are transformed, and here is what is amazing: many times, those around us become interested in what has happened to us. In fact, they may even want to know how their lives can be transformed as well. A change in our lives cannot help but influence those around us.

On the flip side, when we do not change, we can be a stumbling block to others in our lives who know of our faith in Jesus.

Transforming Others

Bearing fruit means changing the lives of others. One of the results of following Jesus is that we help others choose to follow Him as well. We are so moved by what God has done in our lives that we cannot help but share with others what God has done for us. We are motivated by a care and concern for others that compels us to help them discover what we have found in a relationship with God. When we help others choose to follow Christ, we bear fruit. We have multiplied ourselves. We give birth to spiritual children. Embedded into our spiritual DNA is a calling to "go and make disciples" (Matthew 28:18). Jesus once told his disciples, "I chose you to bear fruit—fruit that will last" (John 15:16). Bearing fruit means leading others to follow Jesus.

Paul once wrote to the Romans that he planned to visit them "in order that I might have a harvest among you, just as I have had among the other Gentiles" (Romans 1:13). Paul saw himself as having a major role and responsibility for God's plan in the world. In fact, he defended his authority as an apostle by reminding his doubters about the fruits of his efforts: lives were changed, multiethnic churches were planted, all while Paul served with integrity and suffered greatly to advance the message of Jesus.

We are also called to bear fruit in our relationships. Jesus changes our lives so that we might be his ambassadors in helping others change as well. We are called to impact those we know and love by helping them discover the love of God and a relationship with Jesus.

We can never force anyone to make the same decisions and commitments we have made. God has given us all the freedom to choose a life that excludes or includes His presence. We must have the same attitude.

For a moment, think about the person who has either helped you follow Jesus or who has influenced you to consider faith.

Maybe it was the person who gave you this book! Have you ever considered that God loves you so much that He brought that person into your life to encourage you on your journey?

Now consider this: God loves your coworkers, neighbors, family, and friends so much that He brought you into their lives to help them along in their journey.

We can be a part of pursuing others with God's love. We have the privilege of serving God as His messengers. We can share the life-changing message of Jesus with others so that their lives would be just as transformed as ours. We are to bear fruit by making disciples.

BECOMING RECEPTIVE:
OVERCOMING A HARD HEART

While a large crowd was gathering and people were coming to Jesus from town after town, he told this parable: "A farmer went out to sow his seed. As he was scattering the seed, some fell along the path; it was trampled on, and the birds ate it up...

When he said this, he called out, "Whoever has ears to hear, let them hear."

His disciples asked him what this parable meant. He said, "The knowledge of the secrets of the kingdom of God has been given to you, but to others I speak in parables, so that, "'though seeing, they may not see; though hearing, they may not understand.'

"This is the meaning of the parable: The seed is the word of God. Those along the path are the ones who hear, and then the devil comes and takes away the word from their hearts, so that they may not believe and be saved. (Luke 8:4-5, 8-12, NIV)

GOD SPEAKS. The problem is that too often we are not listening.

Too often we come to closure too soon on who we think God is or what God wants to do in our lives. We need to be open-minded when it comes to God.

We can learn how to be receptive by knowing God personally and discerning how to hear His voice.

Beyond Limitations

Many of us live as defined by our limitations. These limitations are imposed upon us by others or adopted by us. Our future is limited by what others tell us and what we begin to believe about ourselves. As a result, we live "normal," mediocre lives, unable or perhaps unwilling to experience life at our full capacity.

It's in middle school and high school that we seem to struggle most with discovering who we are. We try so hard to fit in that we lose ourselves trying to become like others. We take on the identity of our group, our clique. Growing up in the 80s, we had our popular jocks and cheerleaders, the band geeks, the choir and drama nerds, the New Wavers who listened to The Cure, or the Ropers who wore Cowboy boots. We all seemed to be so desperate to belong that we would try to become someone we weren't.

But have we made much progress since junior high?

So often we pretend to be someone we aren't, and people still don't like us. Think of how much time and energy we have wasted trying to please people who will never be pleased with us!

Rather than limiting our future by focusing on the limitations imposed on us, we can see the future clearly when instead we consider the possibilities as God sees us.

Discovering our calling frees us from these imposed limitations and gives us clarity.

The dictionary defines "becoming" as "any process of change." According to the philosopher Aristotle, "becoming" is any change from the lower level of potentiality to the higher level of actuality.

God offers to guide us toward His ways and toward His purposes, which are beyond what we would imagine and may not be what we expect.

Hiding or Seeking?

One of my favorite games as a child was hide and seek.

I loved to hide and find the absolute best spot where no one could possibly find me. If I did it right, the seeker and all of the other kids hiding were left scratching their heads wondering where I was, even as it was time for the next game to start. Those were the best moments!

It's all fun and games as a child, but often as adults this is how we end up interacting with others. We avoid any unnecessary contact with others. We numb ourselves to relationships by living in a virtual world. With the threat of disease being spread by asymptomatic carriers, everyone is suspect. And then right when you start to open to a relationship with a new friend, they post something online that reveals they are on the other side of a political or social issue than you.

Do you play hide and seek in your relationships or are you receptive to others?

We often hide in our relationships to give off the perception we have it all together more than we actually do. Other times we hide in our relationships because we fear being honest, concerned with what others will think about us. Other times we are available only when we need something from those closest to us, rather than being available for them.

Sometimes we call this "playing hard to get." This may be effective in some situations with dating, but other times we struggle to trust people or risk a relationship to avoid getting hurt. Other times, we don't seem to want to make room for anyone else. Certainly, we need to have healthy boundaries, but do you intentionally make it difficult for others to get close to you? In your relationships, do you really want others to know you?

Here's how you know:

- Have you ever been mad or hurt by a friend, yet you were unwilling to let them know how you felt?
- Have you ever felt lonely, but instead of reaching out to someone, you isolated yourself instead?
- Have you ever found yourself in a dark place, but you were unwilling to reach out for help?

Have you ever found yourself playing hide and seek with God?

I am not sure where you are in your spiritual journey, but most children believe in God when they are young—whether your parents took you to a church on Sunday or not. It is usually when we become teenagers that we start to wonder about God and wander away from God.

Maybe you found yourself in a tough predicament and you prayed for help, but you didn't feel like He was there for you the way you wanted.

Maybe you've seen so much evil in this world, it is hard to believe in a loving God.

Terrible things happen in life. In those moments, we can choose to go to God and others for help, or we can choose to reject God and others. When we push God and others away, our hearts get harder and harder.

Maybe you feel good about your relationship with God, but you know there have been times when you felt so much closer to Him. Perhaps while you were at a camp or on a mission trip, you felt so close to God and to others, but then you went back home, and it all slipped away.

Sometimes God feels far away from us, and we aren't sure why or how that happened or how to feel close to Him again.

Is this all there is? Is more even possible? Let me ask you a deeply personal question: Do you really want to be found? Have you played hard to get with God? If you are unsure about God, would you really want to know if He is there? If you believe in God, are you truly receptive to what He wants for your life?

Hiding in the midst of a childhood game is absolutely fun and acceptable and the entire point of the game. But in real life, hiding from God and from others actually hurts us; at best, it keeps us from becoming all we could be.

Here's the catch: in high school and college we make some of the most important decisions of our lives. Now is the time to be serious about a relationship with God! The beauty of a relationship with God remains the fact that regardless of our age, we can always restart.

Believe it or not—God is not playing hard to get. All too often, we are the ones who are playing games.

A Relationship with God

Throughout the Scriptures, a relationship with God is compared to our relationships with others. Our relationship with God can be "closer than a brother" (Proverbs 18:24). God expresses Himself as a friend (John 15:15) and as a loving Father (John 1:12-13). Even marriage gives us a glimpse at how close God can be to those who want Him to be close, as the Church is referred to as the "Bride of Christ."

I realize some of us have not had healthy relationships with our brother, our friends, or our father, or we haven't seen what a healthy marriage could be like. It is hard to understand what a meaningful relationship with God is like when we cannot understand what a meaningful relationship with anyone is like.

But consider the best moments you've had with others.

- Maybe it was laughing during lunch with a friend at school.
- Maybe it was playing football with your brother as a kid.
- Maybe it was crying on the shoulder of your closest friend.
- Maybe it was a moment when you knew your mom or dad was there for you.

Those best moments with a brother, friend, father, or spouse pale in comparison with the kind of relationship God offers us through Jesus. A meaningful relationship with God means we have access to His love, joy, peace, and presence all day, every day!

One year I was a guest speaker at a leadership conference at a church in Toronto. Personally, I had been working through the Twelve Steps and had found a great deal of healing from anxiety and issues with anger. That whole process helped me feel God's presence more than ever before. It was like for the first time my head and my heart were connected.

After sharing some of the same thoughts about hiding from God or seeking God, the lead pastor came up for a time of Q&A. I was ready for questions on leadership or our ministry in Austin, and then the pastor threw a curve ball when he asked, "You mentioned connecting to God personally, being lost and then found. For those who do not know, what is it like to be found?"

Suddenly, I couldn't speak. Overwhelmed with emotion, tears came to my eyes. Finally, I mumbled my answer to his question: "How do you put into words what it feels like to experience forgiveness? How do you explain what it's like to be loved unconditionally? How can you describe what it's like to discover your life has purpose? How can you communicate what it's like to see God's power demonstrated?"

We were created on purpose and with a purpose. God desires that we experience His love and help others do the same. He wants us to trust and follow Him and help others do the same.

God's plan for us may not always include what we want, but we can always trust Him. In this broken and messed up world, people will use their freedom to do evil—even evil against you and me. God grieves and mourns with us, and God can redeem us when we let Him. He can bring good out of the evil around us when we let Him—when we trust Him.

God is so amazing and so forgiving. And so patient and so good that when we return to Him, He can bring good out of the bad we have done. He can redeem what we destroyed. He can heal what we have broken. Sometimes it may happen in an instant. Sometimes it may take time. Sometimes we still have circumstances that are not what we'd like them to be, but He is with us in those places. We are not alone.

God is there for us.

Here's a promise from the Scriptures:

Come near to God and he will come near to you. (James 4:8, NIV)

A phrase that is found in seven different places in the Old Testament describes God's availability and character like this:

Return to the Lord your God, for he is gracious and compassionate, slow to anger and abounding in love, and he relents from sending calamity. (Joel 2:13, NIV)

Maybe this kind of relationship with God has never been a part of your life. Today, you can get started. You can come near to Him. You can return to the One who created you for a relationship with Him.

Maybe you've had a glimpse of this in the past. You grew up going to church services, but it was your parents' faith. Maybe you have heard the phrase, "God doesn't have any grandchildren." In other words, each of us must choose if we are willing to be adopted by our heavenly Father. We cannot live vicariously through our parents or our friends or our spouse or our pastor.

Jesus came to rescue humanity because we need Him.

If we think we have done enough good to outweigh the bad, then we aren't in a position of receiving all Jesus has done for us. If we know how to answer all the Bible trivia questions, but we do not have a relationship with Jesus, we are missing what God has for us.

During his last meal with his disciples, Jesus explained the very essence of eternal life—the life we all long for and desperately need.

> And this is eternal life: that people know you, the only true God, and that they know Jesus Christ, the One you sent. (John 17:3, NIV)

Getting Closer to God

God is not far away. He is with us, but we will only find Him when we draw near to Him.

God is seeking us, but too often we are hiding.

The letter written by James, one of the leaders in the early church and the half-brother of Jesus, gives insights into why our relationships with others lack intimacy. Our greed and selfishness keep us from getting close to others or to God. We look to others to meet the needs only God can meet. As a result, we are always frustrated with others *and* with God.

> Say a quiet *yes* to God and he'll be there in no time. Quit dabbling in sin. Purify your inner life. Quit playing the field. Hit bottom, and cry your eyes out. The fun and games are over. Get serious, really serious. Get down on your knees before the Master; it's the only way you'll get on your feet. (James 4:7-10, MSG)

So much insight and so much promised to us! Often we don't feel close to God because we don't want to. We are playing hide and seek with God and hoping he does not find us!

When we seek God, we will find Him. When we ask for mercy and forgiveness, we will receive it. When we humble ourselves and admit we need His help, He will lift us up!

God is right here hiding in plain sight!

Did you hear that scientists recently discovered an animal that had never been classified before? This is huge news! Scientists seem to discover new bacteria, new insects, and maybe even new deep-sea amoebas, but finding an animal is quite extraordinary! This new animal has been described as a mix of a cat and a teddy bear face. It's called an olinguito.

Here's what is fascinating. We actually had an olinguito in captivity for years and never realized it.

In an Associated Press article, Seth Borenstein wrote:

> Imagine a mini-raccoon with a teddy bear face that is so cute it's hard to resist, let alone overlook. But somehow science did —until now. . . . The critter leaps through the trees of mountainous forests of Ecuador and Colombia at night, according to a Smithsonian researcher who has spent the past decade tracking them. But the adorable olinguito shouldn't have been so hard to find. One of them once lived in the

Smithsonian-run National Zoo in Washington for a year in a case of mistaken identity.

The little zoo critter, named Ringerl, was mistaken for a sister species, the olingo. Before she died in 1976, Ringerl was shipped from zoo to zoo. . . to try to get it to breed with other olingos. She wouldn't.

"It turns out she wasn't fussy," (zoologist Dr. Kristofer) Helgen said. "She wasn't the right species." Helgen later led a team to South America in 2006.

"When we went to the field we found it on the very first night," said study co-author Roland Kays of the North Carolina Museum of Natural Sciences. "It was almost like it was waiting for us."

In another article, Jane O'Brien of BBC News quoted Dr. Helgen as saying: "This reminds us that the world is not yet explored, and the age of discovery is far from over. The olinguito makes us think—what else is out there?"

My hope is that it's Bigfoot!

For years the olinguito went unnoticed and undetected though it was right there hiding in plain sight the whole time.

If we're not careful, we can make the same mistake and miss the God who is never far from us and is, in that sense, hiding in plain sight.

Move Toward Your Doubt

So if we want healthy relationships with others, and we want a healthy relationship with God, what do we do?

When we connect deeply with God, He can help us connect deeply with others. God is right here with us, even if we don't see Him or feel Him or notice Him.

There is a story at the beginning of the New Testament in Mark 9 of a father whose son was extremely troubled.

Jesus asked the boy's father, "How long has he been like this?"

"From childhood," he answered. . . . "But if you can do anything, take pity on us and help us."

"'If you can'?" said Jesus. "Everything is possible for one who believes."

Immediately the boy's father exclaimed, "I do believe; help me overcome my unbelief!" (Mark 9:21-24, NIV)

Maybe you want to believe but find it difficult. Try the father's prayer: "Jesus, help me overcome my unbelief! Help me believe!"

God can give you the gift of faith. Be honest with your doubts and fears. He can help you believe! I have seen this work time and time again.

You can choose to remain skeptical, or you can try it. Tell God you want to try for one week to live as if you believed He was closer than you think. For one week, you will accept miracles as miracles (rather than coincidences). You will let Him help you trust Him. Just try it for one week!

Doubts can be a path toward greater faith. Don't let doubts scare you away from God. Take those doubts to God and to those a step ahead of you in their spiritual journey. Allow doubts to remind you that you are a spiritual person with questions that can draw you closer to God.

In *The Great Good Thing: A Secular Jew Comes to Faith in Christ*, author and screenwriter named Andrew Klavan writes:

"If you believe, the evidence is all around you.
    If you don't believe, no evidence can be enough."

Too often, we don't see the remarkable because we are too

busy looking for the explainable. We miss the extraordinary because we are looking for the ordinary. We look for the predictable because we want to be in control—but God is unpredictable!

God is pursuing us! He reveals Himself through creation, in history, through the Scriptures, through others who have come into our lives and pointed us toward Him, through signs, through His Spirit, and in so many other ways. God reveals Himself within our hearts when we sense there is more to this life!

Do you want to be found? We tend to wander away even though He is right here pursuing us!

We need to ask God to reveal Himself. We must pursue Him and open our hearts and eyes to see Him in a new way. Be persistent in your pursuit of God. Like any other relationship, it takes effort to grow.

A Persistent Pursuit

In 2003, I discovered how persistent pursuit can pay off. The movie *Finding Nemo* was released. Caleb was four, and Trevi was one.

McDonald's was offering *Finding Nemo* toys with every Happy Meal. Somehow Caleb saw a commercial and wanted to go to McDonald's to "Find Nemo," so we took him.

Well, every time we went to McDonald's, Nemo was never there. Instead, we got Bloat. We got Peach. We got Dory. We got Gill. We got Jacques. We got every single one of them—except Nemo. Despite our inability to find Nemo, Caleb would not give up. Every time we saw a McDonald's, he would plead for us to go so he could find Nemo.

I was so tired of eating at McDonald's! I was living out *Super Size Me* before the documentary had even came out.

Soon we discovered that Nemo had come out during the first week. We had begun our search on week two.

But Caleb remained relentless in his search.

We had a road trip from Los Angeles to Santa Cruz where I was speaking at a youth camp. Every time he saw a McDonald's, he begged us to go. Do you know how many McDonald's restaurants there are between Los Angeles and Santa Cruz? Too many to count!

By the time we went on the trip, I had discovered that McDonald's would let you buy the toy without the entire Happy Meal. None of the McDonald's along that journey from LA to Santa Cruz had a Nemo. We could not find Nemo!

We finally made it into Santa Cruz when Caleb saw another McDonald's. I was tired of going in. Tired of searching for Nemo. He could stay lost as far as I was concerned!

Caleb begged us. I explained to him that we couldn't keep going to all these McDonald's looking for Nemo. Then I noticed something strange. Caleb started talking to himself—or so I thought. I said, "Caleb, what are you doing?" He explained, "I'm asking Jesus to help us find Nemo."

My heart sank. I just knew Caleb's faith would be shattered at the age of four. Nemo seemed nowhere to be found. I tried to let him down gently before we went in. As I asked at the register if they had any Nemo toys, Caleb started jumping up and down: "There's Nemo! There's Nemo!" Well, they didn't have a Nemo toy behind the register, but they had Nemo as part of the entire set to be given away to the winner of a special drawing.

I pleaded with the employee to let me buy the Nemo. When that didn't work, I asked if I could buy the entire set. I assured him he could call the corporate headquarters to get an entire new set or at least a new Nemo before the giveaway, but please, let me have that Nemo!

He would not give in to my desperate plea for help, but he

did let us enter the drawing: one entry per person. All four of us entered, and we left quite dejected.

A few days went by at the youth retreat when we decided to go to another McDonald's near the campground. Why not, right? By now, we were all addicted to the food!

Miraculously, this random McDonald's outside Santa Cruz had a Nemo toy! We were all so excited. We had finally found Nemo! I reminded Caleb that God had answered his prayer. Peace and harmony were back in the universe—or at least in our family. God had helped us finally find Nemo!

Later that day, my phone started ringing. Not knowing who it was, I picked it up. It was the McDonald's in Santa Cruz notifying us that Caleb Bryant had won the entire set of *Finding Nemo* toys!

Now, that was a real miracle!

We never opened the set that he won. He already had a Nemo to play with. I kept the set to sell on eBay one day to help put Caleb through college.

Here's my point: I honestly believe God answered my son's prayer. It was amazing that he won the entire set of Nemo toys.

But was it truly miraculous that we found Nemo? We prayed and we prayed, and we prayed, but we also asked, sought, and knocked on the doors of fifty different McDonald's restaurants trying to find Nemo.

Sometimes God says "yes" to our prayer requests for small things so we can trust Him when He does not answer the way we want on the big things.

Sometimes God says "yes" when we refuse to stop asking.

Sometimes God provides when we refuse to stop looking.

Sometimes God helps us when we are willing to become the answer to our own prayer.

Are we willing to get serious about seeking God?

Are we willing to work on developing a healthy relationship with God and a healthy relationship with others?

Even when God says "no" to our prayers or "not yet" to our prayers, are we willing to trust Him?

In his book, *Prayer: Experiencing Awe and Intimacy with God,* Dr. Timothy Keller writes "God always answers your prayers in precisely the way you want them to be answered if you knew everything he knew."

We need to stop hiding and start seeking God and seeking help from others. We can find favor when we seek after God and when we seek to follow His ways.

True Surrender

Do you ever feel like there are things in your life that are just too big for you? I mean, as you live your life, do you ever find yourself looking square into the face of something that seems so overwhelming that you feel as though you lack the courage or the strength to confront it. It could be any number of things, but the bottom line is that for many, if not most of us, there are times in our lives when we face things that are very intimidating . . . even frightening.

That is the best place to be to experience God's love and power in your life.

This is the exact best place to be to move toward who we want to be and away from the parts of us we don't want to be anymore.

Consider this verse:

You see, at just the right time, when we were still powerless. . . .
(Romans 5:5, NIV)

How could it ever be a good time to be powerless? I am all about forging your own destiny, but there are times when things happen you cannot control and you are caught off guard.

Here's the thing: Admitting we are powerless is when we are

the most honest and the most aware of who we are and the needs we have.

Here's what can happen when we acknowledge we are powerless:

> You see, at just the right time, when we were still powerless, Christ died for the ungodly. Very rarely will anyone die for a righteous person, though for a good person someone might possibly dare to die. But God demonstrates his own love for us in this: While we were still sinners, Christ died for us. (Romans 5:6-8, NIV)

We cannot experience the fullness of God's love until we invite Him into our lives. Admitting we are powerless, admitting we are overwhelmed, admitting we are stuck, moves us to a place of humility where we ask for help. He cannot help if we are too stubborn or too proud to ask for help.

Some of us are bent toward belief, and our struggle is that we believe everything. Some of us are bent toward doubt, and we are cynical about everything.

We can trust God. We can surrender to Him. He has good for us. He can bring good out of the bad.

True surrender is simply to acknowledge the following:

- I am powerless.
- God is powerful.
- I need God.

When we are receptive to God and ready for His help, we can discover the path He has for us.

The Way of Wisdom

Do you ever wonder about the future? Ever worry about the future? Ever feel overwhelmed with all the decisions needing to be made? From the trivial to the life-altering, we are bombarded every day with decisions!

On top of that: How do we know what is God's best for us? He's invisible and seemingly silent! How can we communicate with God to know His design for our lives when we have a hard time communicating with the people in our own home?

The key is to pursue God and His ways rather than just wanting Him to bless our ways. God's will and our wills are intended to work together to make the best decisions, and we can live with confidence that we're making the best decisions for our lives.

The Scriptures paint a picture of a God who created you on purpose and for a purpose.

- Acts 17 tells us that He created us at the exact time in history and put us in the exact part of the planet that gives us the best opportunity to find Him.
- Psalm 139 tells us that God created each of us in our mother's womb and knows all the days set before us.
- Jeremiah 29 tells us that God knows the plans He has for His people, plans to prosper and not to harm.

To experience the life God has for us means to walk in the way of wisdom. There are entire books of the Bible devoted to wisdom, plus the entire Scriptures are filled with case studies of people from whom we can learn. We can learn from their mistakes and from the times they got it right.

King Solomon, one of the wisest people to ever live, said the following:

The fear of the Lord is the beginning of wisdom. (Proverbs 1:7, NIV)

What does that mean? Why would we fear a loving God?

If you met the Creator of the Universe, fear seems like a totally acceptable response! Even still, His awesome power should not keep us away from Him but should compel us to draw near to Him and trust His ways more than our own. He revealed Himself as a man so that we might be able to relate to Him more easily.

Even so, some of us have an unhealthy fear of God. We have an inaccurate view of God that if we do or do not do certain things, God will zap us or block us or be out to get us. In reality, He gives us freedom and responsibility, which means there are consequences for our actions. Often when we think God is being cruel in the Bible, He's actually showing His love by warning us.

If you grew up in a religious context like I did in Texas, it's hard not to get this confused. You see, religion is often our attempt to do good things to appease an angry God.

Appeasing an Angry God?

Some of us may have read part of the Old Testament or heard others talk about the Old Testament as if the God represented in the Old Testament is angry and vengeful and full of wrath, far different than the way Jesus represented God in the New Testament.

It is true that God is going to make all things right on what is called "the Day of the Lord." One day, there will be justice, but God's loving character has never changed.

Throughout the Scriptures that Jesus studied (the Old Testament), a phrase is used nine times to describe God's character: "The Lord is compassionate and gracious, slow to anger, abounding in love" (Psalm 103:8). This phrase was used by God when He revealed His name to Moses in the burning bush in Exodus 34

We discover that God's heart for all people from all nations was evident from the beginning and can be seen throughout the history of the people of Israel as depicted in the Old Testament. In Genesis 12, God chose Abraham and blessed him so that he would be a blessing to all nations. Abraham's family came to be known as the people of Israel. They were a peculiar people with laws and standards like no other people in the ancient world. They were called to be holy, just as they followed their holy God. At times they brought justice as they followed their just God.

In an uncivilized world where every tribe had a god, and each god was seen to be only as strong as the armies representing them, the people of Israel became the most powerful tribe on the planet. People would come to Israel to worship the God of Israel. They would come to see the temple where God lived.

Unfortunately, Israel's renown was short-lived. The nation began to go down the path of trying to appease the angry gods of their neighbors rather than remaining faithful to the compassionate and gracious God who is slow to anger and abounding in love. Rather than being a blessing to all the nations by pointing them toward God, they became just like the other nations.

As a result, God sent His Son to fulfill what Israel was unwilling to do. Jesus lived a perfect and holy life (unlike anyone before Him or anyone since), only to be arrested and tried by religious and political leaders who felt threatened by Him. As a result, He was crucified on a cross. The religious and political leaders thought they had ended Jesus' influence, but they were unaware of the bigger picture. In dying on the cross, Jesus was taking on the sins and wickedness of humanity so that we might be able to share in His holiness. He defeated sin and death. We can now enter the presence of a holy and majestic and perfect

God, because when we surrender our lives to Christ, His death counts for us.

After Jesus rose from the dead and ascended into heaven, the temple was destroyed, as He had predicted. God no longer lived in a place; now He lived within the people who surrendered themselves to Him. We no longer needed to make sacrifices for forgiveness, because Jesus was the ultimate sacrifice. We no longer needed a priest to speak on our behalf to God, because those who follow Jesus are now priests in this new kingdom, able to access God directly.

Once the Messiah came, the kingdom would no longer be limited by geography, but would expand throughout the world. The Messiah's kingdom would no longer be political, but spiritual. The Messiah's kingdom would not require a person to follow the religious rituals of the Jews, but people from every background could now have a relationship with God.

So, what do we do with this idea of God's wrath and judgment? How can that be consistent with a loving and forgiving Jesus?

In John Mark Comer's book *God Has A Name*, in which he breaks down the name of God revealed in Exodus 34, Comer writes:

> But for the writers of the Bible, as well as teachers like Jesus, this cataclysmic 'day of Yahweh' is a bad thing, or a good thing, depending on where you stand with God.
>
> If you're the righteous—the man or woman in right relationships, with God, humanity, and the earth itself—then you can't wait for judgment. Especially if you're the oppressed. Finally, all the world will be set right.
>
> But if you're the wicked, the oppressor, if you refuse Yahweh and his mercy, if you say no to his way of life—then this day should stand as a terrifying warning.
>
> Because God isn't mean, but he is dangerous. Like gravity

or nuclear power or a hurricane—you want to make sure you're on the right side of things. . . . One day God will act decisively to put an end to evil forever. But in the meantime, God's way of dealing with sin is usually to step back and let it run itself into the ground. It turns out that sin is its own punishment, and obedience its own reward.

Reversing the Curse

What the Scriptures show us is that a loving God came to rescue us. We do not need to do good things to make Him like us. He already likes us, and He loves us. It is out of gratitude that we do good things. It is out of gratitude that we walk in God's way of wisdom rather than try to do things on our own. These good things that we do out of gratitude are God's will for our lives.

We make bad decisions when we see something that is not ours and take it. At the root of most bad decisions is our selfishness. Rather than fearing or trusting God, we take what is not intended for us.

Like we see in Genesis with Adam and Eve, they saw what was forbidden and took it anyway. So, Adam and Eve lost their innocence and realized their nakedness. They hid from God because they were ashamed and afraid of Him. They feared God after they made the wrong decision.

Ironically, if they had feared God *before* eating from the tree, then there would have been no need for fearing God *after* eating from the tree. So why did Adam and Eve have to go and ruin everything? I mean, we could have lived naked in paradise, but they had to eat from the one tree they were not allowed to eat! They had complete freedom to eat whatever they wanted, and there were a lot of other trees. But, no, they ate from the one tree they were not allowed to touch!

As a result, humanity was separated from God. We now live under the curse of sin and death. Our rebellion brought death into paradise and brokenness to creation. Our world is cursed. Humanity is cursed. We are cursed. Childbirth is painful. Work is a constant struggle. Men and women try to control and dominate each other. Everything has been affected by that decision to go our way instead of God's way.

The story of the Bible tells us that Jesus' death on the cross restored us back to Eden.

> Christ redeemed us from the curse of the law by becoming a curse for us, for it is written: "Cursed is everyone who is hung on a pole." He redeemed us in order that the blessing given to Abraham might come to the Gentiles through Christ Jesus, so that by faith we might receive the promise of the Spirit. (Galatians 3:13-14, NIV)

Jesus reversed the curse!

We are no longer under the curse because Jesus took the curse on Himself!

We do not have to fall victim to spiritual warfare!

We do not have to have a battle in our homes between women and men!

We do not have to hate our work!

We can walk with God without shame!

We can even have epidurals!

We can experience a glimpse of Eden (heaven on earth)!

We are in Christ and the Spirit of Christ is in us!

Notice what that means:

> "Who has known the mind of the Lord so as to instruct him?" But we have the mind of Christ. (1 Corinthians 2:9-16, NIV)

This is remarkable! We have the mind of Christ—the wisdom of God!

As followers of Jesus, He told us to pray:

"Father, Your Kingdom come, your will be done on earth as it is in heaven!"

So, what does that mean for decision-making?

We should be making decisions that reverse the curse! We live differently than the ways of this broken world. We live holy lives with God's help. We work toward unity and peace in our homes. Our homes should be places where men, women, and children know they are loved and valued and have a way to contribute. Our place of work brings us and others joy. We should be making decisions that bring more of a glimpse of heaven to earth!

It's not just what is best for me. It's not just what feels best. It's not just what's easiest or most convenient. These are concerns that our world tells us matter.

In *Decision Making and the Will of God*, Gary Friesen and J. Robin Maxson point out that God's guidance according to the way of wisdom can be summarized in four simple statements:

1. "Where God commands, we must obey."

Do you know what God wants for us? His Word to us is clear through the Scriptures, also known as the Word of God! God makes clear His moral will for us. There are so many things that are so clearly described.

2. "Where there is no command, God gives us freedom (and responsibility) to choose."

In my freedom, I don't go against the moral will of God, nor do I cause others to stumble. In my freedom, I choose to serve others. I seek to become a person of integrity, making the right decision, no matter how small it is, and even when no one is looking.

This also means when you have more than one good choice, you don't have to be paralyzed with fear or uncertainty, thinking only one of the good choices is right. With God's help, you can make whichever good option you choose work.

3. "Where there is no command, God gives us wisdom to choose."

So walk in the way of wisdom! We are not supposed to be in this alone!

4. "When we have chosen what is moral and wise, we must trust the sovereign God to work all the details together for good."

There is still mystery, but God is not hiding from us. He wants us to do His will more than we do. He is speaking, but too often we are not listening.

When you are walking with God, you have lots of great options and opportunities. Like Adam and Eve, we can eat of any tree, but we are to avoid taking what is not ours. When we choose to fear, trust, obey, and delight in God, and we allow all other decisions to flow from that relationship, God will guide us.

When making decisions, we need to ask ourselves: "Is this showing others the love of God? Is this demonstrating loving others? Does this decision help advance the message of Jesus around me? With this decision, am I reversing the curse?"

Come Back to Texas?

Now, I have never heard God's voice audibly, but I have heard Him speak to me in many remarkable ways.

Sometimes God invites us to do things we do not want to do. As a result, we do not hear Him speak because we are ignoring Him. Either we are afraid to trust Him, or we don't want to do what He wants us to do, or we don't want to stop doing what we are doing because we like it!

I've been there. My wife, kids, and extended family all wanted us to live in Texas. My wife, Deborah, and I both grew up in Texas. All our family is there. After fifteen years of us living on the West Coast, they all wanted us to move. There was only one person standing in the way: me. I didn't want to leave Los Angeles. I liked what I was doing and where we were living.

At a family get-together out at Lake LBJ, I heard my mom, my aunt (who lives in Austin), my wife, and my daughter all talking about how they were praying we would move to Texas. That was the final straw for me! I was so frustrated with them. They were praying something would happen in my life that I did not want to happen!

As we drove back to Los Angeles, Deborah and I spent those three days talking about our future. It was on that trip that I agreed to at least pray and ask God what He wanted us to do—which before had been something I had been resistant to do.

On the day I was supposed to begin praying about whether we should stay in LA or move to Texas, I decided to go to the gym. (This was the first miracle. I rarely went to the gym.) As I walked in, I noticed how loud the music seemed to be that early in the morning. Despite that, I prayed quietly in my mind: "God, just guide me to know where you want us to live—where you want us to serve you." It was at that moment that I heard this song:

"Come back to Texas
It's just not the same since you went away
Before you lose your accent
And forget all about the Lone Star State
There's a seat for you at the rodeo
And I've got every slow dance saved
Besides the Mexican food sucks north of here anyway"

It was a song I had never heard before and have never heard on the radio since. I later discovered it was the same guys who sing the theme song to the cartoon Phineas and Ferb, a band called Bowling for Soup. The name of the song is "(Ohio) Come Back to Texas."

Honestly, I was a bit freaked out—so much so that when I got on the treadmill and noticed that ESPN was showing highlights from a Little League game with California versus Texas, I just couldn't take it anymore. I told God: "This is too much for me. Just make it clear where we are supposed to go. Whoever wins this game is where we will live!" Then the Texas team won.

After several amazing events and crazy circumstances that seemed to confirm a move, my wife changed her mind—and didn't want to move. Crisis averted!

A year later, I started to think we were supposed to be moving. Strange things started happening again, so I initiated the possibility with Deborah. One moment in particular came when I was reading from Ezekiel:

> "I am sending you to an obstinate and stubborn people. . . . You are not being sent to a people of obscure speech and difficult language.... Go now to your countrymen. . . ." (Ezekiel 2:4, 3:5,11)

Doesn't that sound like Texas? A stubborn and obstinate people! I am a Texan, and these words described me. "Countrymen"! And what other state in America thinks of itself as its own country?

So much more happened that I don't have time to include, but the adventure of moving to Austin and serving as part of Gateway Church brought us closer to God and closer to each other.

Hearing God's Voice

We can learn to discern God's voice in our lives when we develop a posture of receptivity. We can move from a hardened heart to a vulnerable one.

Every follower naturally should hear His voice. Jesus once said:

> "My sheep listen to my voice; I know them, and they follow me." (John 10:27, NIV)

A friend of mine contacted me and wanted to learn how to hear God's voice. I was ready to walk him through this same process. As we caught up on each other's lives, he told me about a moment when he woke up and decided to just let go of something he had been trying to make happen that seemed to be going nowhere. I asked him how he knew to just "let go." He paused and answered, "I just knew God wanted me to 'let go.'" Then he said something incredibly profound: "I guess it's not that God isn't speaking to me. I guess He's not saying what I want to hear."

All of us, no matter where we may be in our spiritual journeys, need to be willing to hear the fresh message God has for us.

What are your dreams and hopes for your future? Are these your own dreams, or are these dreams God has for you? Are these selfish dreams, or selfless dreams?

To experience the life God created us to experience, to become who we were created to be, we need to entrust all our hopes, dreams, fears, doubts, and regrets, along with our past, present, and future to God. When we let go of our dreams, God can replace them with His dreams for our lives—which are far more beautiful than what you or I could ever imagine!

When we seek God for wisdom in every area of life, He will guide us.

God's true will for us is to live like Jesus wherever we are and bring him glory whatever we are doing (1 Corinthians 10:31). If we are committed to a sacrificial "way of the cross" type of life, we will do God's will wherever we go.

When it comes to discerning God's voice for specific steps, He may want us to take, we need to remain open-minded and soft-hearted. As we journey through life with God, He gives us clues. He doesn't overwhelm us with all that is ahead; he gives us just enough so we can keep making progress and will keep looking to Him.

God gives us supernatural, external, and internal clues, including the following:

Supernatural Clues

- Seeking God
- Spirit of God
- Signs

External Clues

- Sage counsel
- Circumstances

Internal Clues

- Significance

LET'S walk through these six types of clues.

Supernatural Clues

Sometimes God speaks when we seek Him through the Scriptures, fasting, and prayer.

Let me give you an example. Deborah and I were engaged to be married and were invited to move to Seattle to help plant a church. We began to ask God: "Should we move to Seattle?" To help discern what was best, I then started reading through all that Jesus ever said that was recorded in the Bible, as well as Proverbs and Psalms. I began writing down all the verses that seemed to point us in that direction.

One verse that jumped out at me was from the Gospel of Mark, which says:

> "No one who has left home or brothers or sisters or mother or father or children or fields for me and the gospel will fail to receive a hundred times as much in this present age." (Mark 10:29-30, NIV)

This resonated in my heart as a reminder that God does call us at times to be willing to leave our biological family for the sake of reaching out to others. There were many other passages that all seemed to affirm that God was guiding us to move.

Other times the Spirit of God leaves an impression or thought through what the Scriptures call "a still small voice" (1 Kings 19:12).

We can discern God's voice from our own by realizing that the thoughts we have that are from God are selfless, require courage, and are consistent with His character as shown in the Scriptures.

God can also speak in remarkable ways by using signs, as I shared when describing how we were discerning whether we should move to Texas. It is important to not only look for signs, but also to not completely dismiss them either.

External Clues

An important way God speaks to us is through the wise counsel of others. Seeking out advice from others keeps us connected with others and humble. Both open the way for God to speak.

Scott (the filmmaker in our small group who I mentioned earlier had seen all he hoped for happen and more when it came to his spiritual goals) said this about seeking out relationships with others who follow Jesus: "The more I connected with other believers, the more I felt God's profound presence in my life. And the easier it was to hear his voice and guidance. Through community, God became a living, breathing reality for me."

With humility, we should also consider our circumstances. Nothing should be beneath us. Sometimes God opens a door that requires kneeling to go through. We miss God's leading because we think we are above, beyond, or too good for opportunities offered to us.

Some of us lack the courage to do something new, but some of us lack the character to stay where we are. Our circumstances do not mean we should choose what is easiest, but instead we should consider if God is opening an opportunity in such a way that we need to go through it, or stay, or not.

For example, when considering our move to Seattle, a woman at our church in Waco, Texas, had a niece who lived in Seattle who was willing to let us stay at her place for $75 per month. Going from not having a place to live to having one at such an affordable price was a shift in our circumstances that opened the door toward the move.

Internal Clues

When it comes to internal clues, we should consider our significance. What makes you unique? Consider the desires of your heart, passions, spiritual gifts, strengths, background, and so on.

The Scriptures say that the "prospect of the righteous is joy" (Proverbs 10:28) and that if you "Delight yourself in God, and He will give you the desires of your heart" (Psalm 37:4).

Also, ask yourself: Can anyone else do this? What needs do you see that you can meet? The ability to meet the needs of others in ways that others may not be able to do so, may point toward God's leading. Another way to ask this would be the following: What needs do you see that you are uniquely designed to meet? What is God calling you to do that makes the world a better place?

Jesus sees so much potential in you! He desires to change your life and to allow you to see the lives of those you care about change through your influence!

When we are receptive to knowing God personally and learning to hear His voice, we are on our way to discerning God's design for us to have a fruitful life.

Reflection:

When have you sensed you heard God's voice? What happened?

When have you been hard-hearted toward God's voice? What helped you get out of that mindset?

Are you willing to ask God for help, forgiveness, and guidance on how to move forward, no matter what you may be facing?

Work through the section on "God's Calling" in Appendix A.

BECOMING TENACIOUS:
OVERCOMING TRIALS

"Some fell on rocky places, where it did not have much soil. It sprang up quickly because the soil was shallow. But when the sun came up, the plants were scorched, and they withered because they had no root. . . . The seed falling on rocky ground refers to someone who hears the word and at once receives it with joy. But since they have no root, they last only a short time. When trouble or persecution comes because of the word, they quickly fall away...." (Matthew 13:5-6, 20-21, NIV)

IF GOD IS CALLING us to a life that is transformed and transforming others, we have to develop a deep faith to get there. When we have a shallow faith, we quit too soon. Too often, making progress comes and goes based on our circumstances. We can overcome trials by learning to become tenacious.

Here's how we can become tenacious:

1. Remember who you are.
2. Remember Whose you are.
3. Remember your calling.
4. Redefine success.

Defeating Nazis (and Other Struggles)

Often the challenges we face can get in the way of our efforts to become who we were created to be.

A famous line from Winston Churchill summarizes what should be our response in the midst of trials. He said: "Never, never, never, never give up."

Facing the Nazi threat in Europe and during World War II, Churchill said a great deal of great things that are inspiring for us in the midst of facing trials. A few of my favorites include the following:

"Success is the ability to go from failure to failure without losing your enthusiasm."

"Success is not final. . . Failure is not fatal. . . It's the courage to continue that counts."

"A pessimist sees the difficulty in every opportunity; an optimist sees the opportunity in every difficulty."

"If you're going through hell, keep going."

Comparing what we face to the leadership it took to defeat the Nazis may seem a bit extreme, but we all face trials—big and small. What is a small challenge to some of us may be a big challenge for others of us. Often, we learn from the challenges we face so that we are more prepared for whatever comes our way next. We can also learn from those who have overcome much to help us amid our struggles.

Do you give up when things get tough? Consider your relationships or your career: Do you jump from job to job and from relationship to relationship? If so, you may be living with a shallow faith.

Remember Who You Are

In his book *Unshockable Love,* John Burke writes about how we are created by God to be a masterpiece, but it may be hard to see with all the mud and muck in our lives. Our lives are like a painting found in the dumpster. The masterpiece gets lost in the pain we face. We are all broken and needing grace—just like every other person we meet! Recognizing the hurts and brokenness in our lives is an important element of truly knowing who we are.

Some of the trials we've faced have come in the form of evil people who do evil things. Other times, we face hardships because of the fallen world in which we live. Disease, disasters, and destruction seem to be all around us.

We face challenges that are beyond what we think anyone could ever handle, yet somehow, we are far more resilient than we think.

Over the course of a few weeks, two of our Gateway couples lost their babies. One was a newborn. One was three years old. As we spent time talking, crying, and praying together, I learned something important from them: We may never understand why these tragedies happened, but we can experience the love of God and community acutely in these terrible moments. As John Burke said, "When you have no hope, borrow it from someone else."

When we face trials, we can use the pain as an excuse to walk away from God and walk away from relationships, or we can use the pain to run toward God and run toward relationships.

In a small group in Austin, a couple was sharing with us how they overcame the painful loss of their teenage daughter. She said: "I wanted to push God away. I wanted to push my husband away, but instead I held onto God and grabbed hold of my husband tighter."

When going through the Twelve Steps as a church together, I was encouraged by the Serenity Prayer. The Twelve Steps helped us apply spiritual disciplines to our lives to overcome our struggles, no matter what those might be. You may be familiar with the first part, which reads:

God grant me the serenity
to accept the things I cannot change;
courage to change the things I can;
and wisdom to know the difference.

That is so true and so inspiring and such a great prayer to sincerely pray, but I find the rest and less familiar part just as helpful.

Living one day at a time;
enjoying one moment at a time;
accepting hardships as the pathway to peace;
taking, as He did, this sinful world
as it is, not as I would have it;
trusting that He will make all things right
if I surrender to His will;
that I may be reasonably happy in this life
and supremely happy with Him forever in the next.
Amen.

This world is not the way God intended it, but this is a temporary state. In this broken and messed up world, our hardships can become "the pathway to peace." We can trust Him no matter what may come.

Haunted by The Past

For some of us, we face a trial in the form of a person. There are people in our life who we love who never quite loved us the way we wanted or needed, or we may be haunted by a broken relationship.

Let's take our fathers for instance. Some of us have dads who tried really hard but just couldn't quite pull it off. Others of us had dads who were never there or dads who hurt us some of us. Some of us have dads who were fantastic.

I love my dad. He's a great dad; but we had some tough moments. We didn't quite understand each other.

When I was about eleven years old, I remember coming up to my dad and wanting to give him a hug goodnight, but he told me that I was getting a little bit too old for hugs, so he extended his hand for a handshake. I shook his hand and sadly walked to my room. The good news is that to this day, I have a great firm grip.

When I was in high school, we got into a huge argument because I wanted to grow my hair out long. Ironically, just ten years later I shaved my head and have kept it short ever since. If only he had known then what we all know now.

When my wife and I were engaged, my mom encouraged my fianceé to call her "JoAnne" instead of "Mrs. Bryant." Sitting right next to her, my dad didn't say anything. I found him later and asked: "Why didn't you offer to let her call you 'Pat'?"

He responded, "I don't want her to call me 'Pat.' I want her to call me 'Mr. Bryant.'"

I was surprised and asked, just to make certain I heard him correctly: "So you are wanting my future wife to call you two 'JoAnne and Mr. Bryant'?"

He said: "Yes, it wasn't my idea to give out my first name. Once you start having kids, then she can call me by my grandpa name."

For six years we did not have children, so my wife didn't know what to call my dad. She would just wait until she had eye contact before talking with him.

One of the worst fights we had was the night before the rehearsal dinner for our wedding. I came to my parents' house around 11:00 p.m.. The lights were still on which concerned me because my parents usually fell asleep at 8:00 p.m. watching TV. I knew this was not good. My suspicions were confirmed when I walked into the living room. They were upset. By that point I had lived away from home for four years; I was not used to a curfew. They were upset that I hadn't been there to talk about the rehearsal dinner plans.

My dad started yelling at me: "Why weren't you here? Why don't you care about anyone else but yourself?"

I thought, *If I start yelling louder than him, it will help him see how crazy he is and then he will stop*

So, I started yelling at him. "Well, I didn't know what time you wanted me to come back! How am I supposed to guess what you want from me?"

Even though I had planned to stop yelling after making my point, I did not stop. Our yelling got louder and louder. Our faces kept getting closer and closer. Spit was flying and fists were clenching before we finally went off to our own rooms.

I had some very angry thoughts in that moment. I was thinking about our move to Seattle and how I wouldn't let him come to visit, and I wouldn't be coming back. Then I started rethinking my plan, because I still wanted to see my mom, so I decided that I would let them come to visit once we had kids, but the kids would call him 'Mr. Bryant'!

As I finally started to calm down, I began to get tired. Now, I try to pray every night before I go to sleep, and on this night at first, I prayed a very angry prayer dealing with justice and revenge. The longer I prayed, the more my heart began to change. I realized I probably shouldn't have yelled, and I probably should have told them what time I was coming home. I didn't realize they were anxious about the next night's events. Eventually, I felt compelled to walk across the dark house and apologize to my dad.

The lights were off in their bedroom, but I went in and kneeled beside the bed on the side where he was. I said: "Dad, I'm so sorry. I should have told you what time I was coming home, and I'm sorry I yelled at you. I hope you'll forgive me."

As I got up, my job was done. I was ready to leave. I didn't care if he had heard me or not. It was in that moment I heard a sound I had not heard from my dad very much. I could tell he was crying.

In that moment, he said these words: "I'm just having a hard time saying goodbye."

You see, sometimes hurt people hurt people. It wasn't that my dad didn't care; it was that he didn't know what to do with all the care that he had.

Some of the people in your life may not know how to love you the way you want to be loved.

That night helped me change my perspective. I tried to look backward to remember all the best moments rather than focus on the worst moments. I began to remember how my dad coached my little league baseball team, even though he doesn't like sports. There were moments where he encouraged me to try out for things that I would not likely make. There were moments when he believed in me when no one else did. There were moments when he would get in the car and drive me during one of these crazy winter storms we have in Central Texas so I could get to work. He was willing to do what no one else was willing to do.

In doing so, I began to see things a little bit differently. My dad had one of the most stressful jobs on the planet as an air traffic controller. When most of us make mistakes at work, a couple people might get mad; but if he made a mistake, hundreds of people could die. My dad also comes from a different era. They don't know how to show emotions, and their dads were even worse than them.

Several years ago, I was at my grandmother's house and found this little book from 1967 called *So Many Kinds of Love*. I brought it home to read it to my daughter. It's a cute little book for children that talks about your mom's love, your cat's love, your brother's love, and even talks about your dad's love. It says this: "Your dad has a strong and secure kind of love. He may not tell you that he loves you, but he doesn't need to because you just know."

Back in 1967 I guess the author was trying to lower kids' expectations!

Maybe your dad has come from a different era and doesn't know how to give you what you want from him. Maybe your dad failed you miserably. Maybe you faced abuse from the man who was supposed to care for you.

Whatever your experience, I know your heavenly Father can meet your needs in a way that your earthly dad never could.

Some of us have relationships that have been broken over misunderstandings, unexpressed expectations, or with wounded people who don't know how to love us the way we want. Even still, when you look back at your life, are you focused on the results of the painful moments—the good that came out of those moments—or are you focused on the pain? Do you have grace for those who have hurt you?

Daniel Kahneman won the Nobel Prize in Economics for his pioneering work in behavioral economics. Daniel Kahneman reveals how our "experiencing selves" and our "remembering selves" perceive happiness differently.

The idea is that "being happy about one's life" is very different than "being happy in one's life." We can remember the results of the painful moments or focus on the pain of the experience. For example, if a woman focuses on the results of pregnancy, labor, and childbirth, then she is likely to have a child. She is happy about the memory. If she focuses on what she experienced in labor and delivery, then she may never have another child again.

It is possible to shift your perspective and see that some of the people who hurt you were hurt by others, and you may be the one who experienced their displaced anger.

Do you know who you are? Do you realize how much grace you've been given? Are you willing to extend that same level of grace to others?

I wish I had realized this when I was younger, but one day it dawned on me: God loves my family so much that he put me in it so that I might find God and experience His healing—so that I could bring that healing to everyone in my family who is older than me and to all those who come after me.

> God saved you by his grace when you believed. And you can't take credit for this; it is a gift from God. Salvation is not a reward for the good things we have done, so none of us can boast about it. For we are God's masterpiece. He has created us anew in Christ Jesus, so we can do the good things he planned for us long ago. (Ephesians 2:8-10, NLT)

Learning to Lament

God does not promise a life without struggles. Instead, He promises to be with us in the struggle.

The Bible shows us a way to process our grief, a way to make it through suffering. There is a word common in the Bible we have lost in our culture. It's the word "lament." We need to learn to lament. When we don't, those feelings come out sideways. Lament is not the feeling of grief, but the expression of grief. God invites us to lament.

In fact, there are Psalms of lament and even an entire book

of the Bible called Lamentations, which was written by Jeremiah after Jerusalem was destroyed by the Babylonians. Their capital, their temple, was torn apart, and the people were dragged away into exile.

Dr. Tim Mackie of BibleProject™ describes Lamentations this way: "Suffering in silence is not a virtue in the book of lamentations. God's people are not asked to deny their emotions but voice their protest, to vent their feelings, and pour it out before God. . . . Lament and prayer and grief are a crucial part of the journey of faith of God's people in a broken world."

In January 2020, I attended a course with seminary professor Dr. Gregory Cuellar in Austin. Little did I know how relevant this book would become. He pointed out that, "Lamentations was written from the vantage point of the captive, the victim rather than the victor, who was exposed to hyper-violence and the stench of death."

The first word of the first verse in the first chapter is a word phrase: "How is this?" In other words: "How is this possible? How did this happen?"

Have you ever found yourself feeling that way? When we do, it is important to let yourself grieve. We aren't good with grief or loss. At some point, we need to realize that loss is a part of life. The world is broken, and it will be until God makes all things right one day.

Too often, we have this false belief that if we trust God and do all the right things, then He will give us all the good things in life.

At Gateway Church in Austin, we shared a time of lament for the death of Ahmaud Arbery. Just a couple of weeks later, we had a time of lament to grieve the death of George Floyd. When tragedies happen in our lives and in our country, we need to lament.

As followers of Jesus, it is important to lament and grieve injustice felt by many people of color in our nation and stand with those who want change in our society so that innocent men are not assumed guilty or even killed because of the color of their skin. We need to lament and grieve how peaceful protestors can be lumped in with those who start looting, and we also lament and grieve how a few bad police are casting a dark shadow on the many good law officers who risk their lives to protect. We need to grieve how evil pits whole groups of people, races, professions, against each other as enemies. Sadly, there is so much more injustice that never makes the news and that we don't see because there wasn't a video camera on at the time.

So, we grieve. We lament. And we take action to bring change.

We need to take the time to put into words what we are feeling during the difficult times in life. Amid suffering, it is also important to ask: What have we lost that is a good thing to lose?

Even during the violent destruction of his home, Jeremiah writes of hope:

> Because of the Lord's great love we are not consumed, for his compassions never fail. They are new every morning; great is your faithfulness. I say to myself, "The Lord is my portion; therefore I will wait for him." (Lamentations 3:22-24, NIV)

Waiting is hard. We don't like to wait. Even still, we can survive suffering. God is with us in our pain.

To become tenacious, remember who you are—broken, grieving, and needing grace just like those who have hurt you.

Remember Whose You Are

To become tenacious, you also need to remember Whose you are.

One of the more amazing truths about God remains this: He

chooses us in spite of who we are and what we've done, and when we let Him, He can somehow bring good out of the bad moments in our life.

> And we know that in all things God works for the good of those who love him, who have been called according to his purpose. (Romans 8:28, NIV)

There's that word again: "called." You and I have been called by God—invited by God to follow Him, to experience life and freedom, to become fruitful, to be transformed, and to transform others.

When we say "yes" to our calling—when we say "yes" to following Christ—we become His. We become part of His family—one of the chosen.

For example, in Genesis 12:1-3 God chose Abraham to become the father of a great nation and through Him all nations would be blessed. This is important. By choosing one person, God was choosing all of us.

> "I will make you into a great nation, and I will bless you. . . and you will be a blessing. . . and all peoples on earth will be blessed through you." (Genesis 12:2-3, NIV)

There's great freedom when we know we belong to God. No matter what, He's never going to let us go.

God reveals Himself to us through the person of Jesus and through His Word to us. We can discover His character through how God interacts with humanity, Israel, and the Church in the Bible.

For just a moment, whatever resistance you may be feeling, or whatever your experience has been with the Bible, I want you to consider having an open mind. What if what keeps you from experiencing all the Bible has to offer has more to do with your view of the Bible than the Bible itself?

Some of us have hit a ceiling in our spiritual growth. We think we have arrived, or we think that this is all there is. We need to become more open-minded to the possibility that God has more for us.

To make matters even more complicated, many of us have given up on the Scriptures, haven't understood the Bible, or haven't made spending time in the Scriptures a priority because there are spiritual forces opposing us. The darkness in our hearts, and the darkness in the world around us, does not want us to discover the mysteries that are revealed in the Scriptures.

Paul wrote to the church in the city of Corinth. He reminded them that when we choose to fully surrender our lives and follow Jesus, through the Spirit of God and through God's revelation to us through His Word, we can understand the character of God and even the mind of Christ! His thoughts can become our thoughts! He reminds us that we are those entrusted with the mysteries God has revealed mysteries not to keep hidden, but to share with all who want to know!

Through the stories, poetry, histories, prophecies, and songs written by men and women who encountered God and even spent time with Jesus, God reveals Himself to us. We discover God's character. We discover the best and the worst of humanity. We discover people just like us: broken and messed up, who can experience healing and become heroes for others when they're willing to let God work in their hearts.

To reframe our view of the Scriptures, let me take you back to a simpler time: 1992. That may be before you were born or before you have much of a memory. Or maybe you remember 1992 quite well.

At that point, you did not have to disrobe to make it through airport security. It was also before laptop computers, cell phones, and even before Al Gore invented the Internet.

It was a simpler time. The Dallas Cowboys were poised to win their third, fourth, and fifth Super Bowls. Michael Keaton was Batman. And Will Smith was the Fresh Prince of Bel Air.

Why do I want to take you back to 1992? Why does anyone want to go back in time?

You see, there was a girl.

Isn't it always about a girl?

In particular, it was *my* girl.

Her name was Deborah Ellis. Named after the warrior princess in the Scriptures. She was beautiful, intriguing, and had a heart for God like no one else I had ever met. She was an amazing girl, and I wanted her to be my girl.

There was a problem. She lived in Irving, Texas, and I lived in Waco. She lived 100 miles away. Without the Internet or money to make long-distance phone calls, I pursued her using parchment and pen.

To reach the heart of this girl, I wrote her a letter, placed it in an envelope, and chose a stamp to ensure its delivery.

In those days, we did not call it "snail mail." We simply called it "the mail."

The goal of my letters was to win her heart. The goal of my letters was a relationship with her.

So why share some of this love story? Because our love stories give us a glimpse into the greatest love story of all: God's pursuit of humanity!

Like a love letter, the Bible is designed to connect us to the One who loves us.

My letters to Deborah included poetry and stories about my life, but also stories about others. This way she got to know me and how I treated other people.

Love letters don't just say "I love you" over and over!

So, let's consider what the Bible says about itself:

For the word of God is living and active, sharper than any two-edged sword, piercing to the division of soul and of spirit, of joints and of marrow, and discerning the thoughts and intentions of the heart. (Hebrews 4:12, NIV)

The Bible is never to be used as a weapon to bludgeon people. Instead, the Bible is more like a scalpel that does work on us to heal us from what ails us.

Don't just read the Scriptures; let the Scriptures read you.

We can grow to trust God and His Word fully when we surrender our opinions, our experiences, our preconceived notions, our politics, or *ANYTHING* that we impose on God or on the Scriptures.

The goal of the Scriptures is not to get more information. The goal is transformation—understanding who God is and living a new life under His leadership and with His guidance.

Applying the Bible means trusting God, and trusting God means a real relationship with God. That is the goal of the Scriptures.

I didn't just want Deborah to read my letters and think highly of me or reach out to me just when she was in trouble. I wanted a relationship with her!

Author, speaker, lead pastor at Mosaic in Los Angeles, and one of my mentors, Erwin McManus, puts it this way:

"The Scriptures are a portal into God's presence."

God is reaching out to you and me and revealing Himself through the Scriptures so that you and I might develop a deeper relationship with Him.

If the Bible is new to you, start with the Gospels: the stories of Jesus from Matthew, Mark, Luke, and John. Spend time in the New Testament. Become familiar with the stories. The Old Testament has inspiring stories and many things to apply to our lives, but it was also a time when people anticipated the coming Savior, so there are many laws about the temple, sacrifices, and ceremonies that no longer need to be applied because the Savior has already come.

Seek to understand the context and interpret Scripture with the Scriptures. This will help you avoid some of the pitfalls of reading this ancient and beautiful book and taking things out of context.

As you read the Bible, ask God to speak to you, and then act. When in doubt, ask others who are walking with God to help you understand how to apply what you are discovering.

There are many misconceptions about the Bible, in large part because people have misused and misinterpreted the Bible to advance their own racist or misogynistic agendas. The Bible is not a series of boring stories that have no relevance to our lives. It isn't just a book to read like any other book. It's not pro slavery, misogynistic, prudish about sex, or advocating genocide. Let's tackle just a few of these.

The Bible is not pro slavery. It just so happened that 80 percent of the Roman world and probably even a higher percentage of the early Church were slaves, so the authors of the New Testament were writing to let these slaves know how to live in that environment, even as they advocated for freedom, like in the book of Philemon. Remarkably, in the letters to the churches, Paul is writing to slaves directly. This shows he sees those who are enslaved as people and not as property.

You might think that Paul should call those who were slaves to rise up and rebel (and we know there are times when this would be absolutely the right thing), but the plight of slaves in Paul's day was different than what we think of when we think of the early history of the United States of America, which was race-based chattel slavery. Many of those who were enslaved 2,000 years ago were paying off a debt. They chose servitude to get out of their difficult circumstances. The Hebrew Scriptures called for those who were enslaved to be freed every seven years (which is very different than forced slavery). The early church leaders knew that as people were freed from spiritual slavery, then the end of physical enslavement would soon follow. This is revolutionary!

The Bible is not misogynistic (against women). The Bible and the early followers of Jesus liberated women. In Christ, there is no difference between Jews and Gentiles, slaves and free people, men and women! There is also no distinction between men and women when it comes to receiving spiritual gifts. An often-misunderstood verse mentions that "women should learn in quietness and submissiveness" (1 Timothy 2:11). We have a hard time getting past the "quietness and submissiveness" part to see that Paul was advocating that women should learn in a culture and in a time when women were oppressed and seen as property. There are still some places in our world that do not allow girls to go to school, but those are not nations influenced by Christianity. Another way to see this verse would be more like: "be sure to teach women, but make sure they keep their freedom quiet and orderly so that the patriarchal world does not shut us down."

The Bible is not prudish about sex. There is even a passage that advocates married couples to be intimate often and regularly to protect against the enemy's attacks. The Bible holds sex up as a more intimate and more important experience than our culture does. It is important to come with an open mind, knowing that God calls us to an ideal to protect us, not to stifle us.

The Bible is not advocating genocide. It is hard for us to wrap our heads around the violence in the Hebrew Scriptures, but it's important to remember that many of these events took place 3,000 to 4,000 years ago, in a time very different than our own. It was a time when all the tribes were more like ISIS. It was a brutal time when children were often sacrificed to the gods. There were times when God used the nation of Israel to bring an end to the reign of evil empires, much like the Allies ended the Nazi regime. In the New Testament, we are told that "our battle is not against flesh and blood," so this idea of a holy war ended with Jesus and is not how God works in this world.

The Bible is not just a giant rule book or a giant "Don't Do List." Instead, the Old Testament reveals the covenant relationship between God and His people. As the Zondervan NIV Study Bible puts it: "The law was the way of life for the redeemed, not a way of salvation for the lost." The Old Testament reveals the character and holiness of God, how far we have fallen from Him, and how much we need God to rescue us. The New Testament shows God rescuing us, and His name is Jesus. Knowing the context helps us make sense of the message intended for the original audience, which helps us apply the message to our lives.

The reality is that throughout history all nations informed by Christianity (informed by the Bible) have moved toward having women in leadership and away from slavery. Sure, we still have a long way to go, but the trajectory that began in the Scriptures moves toward value and worth and love beyond what any culture would be like naturally. (There are great resources like BibleProject.com, *The New Testament for Everyone* series by N.T. Wright, and *How (Not) to Read the Bible* by Dan Kimball that I highly recommend for helping understand the context.)

We can grow to know more about God and Whose we are by reading, meditating, memorizing, applying, and praying through the Scriptures. Let the Word of God saturate your heart and mind.

When it comes to remembering Whose we are, God's message for us can be found in Deuteronomy:

Be strong and courageous. Do not be afraid or terrified because of them, for the Lord your God goes with you; he will never leave you nor forsake you. (Deuteronomy 31:6, NIV)

When things get tough, you may not know what to do, but you can know the One who does. You can trust Him. You can trust that somehow what was intended for evil, He can work so powerfully and mysteriously that good can come out of the darkest moments. We do not know why, but we know the One who does. We can trust Him.

We can choose hope even when we don't feel like it.

Remember Your Calling

I am so grateful. So grateful for my parents, my brother, my extended family, my childhood, my education, my opportunities in life, my health, my friends, my wife, my children, my experiences, my church families, my career, my coworkers, my calling, and so much more. I have been so blessed! I am so grateful!

When I am overwhelmed with gratitude, I always think of Jesus' words:

"To whom much is given, much is required." (Luke 12:48)

I have wrestled with what was required of me as someone who was born with so much opportunity and freedom as a white male in America and with parents and grandparents who worked hard to open doors for me.

As a child I had a sense of who God created me to be. You see, I was born the day after Dr. Martin Luther King, Jr. and the day before Andy Kaufman, a comedian popular in the 1970s and early 1980s. His birthday also happens to be the same birthday as Jim Carey, who portrayed him in a film called *Man on the Moon*.

I was not exactly sure what that meant, but I felt I was to be some sort of advocate for others and to make others laugh.

For me, I found a sense of my calling in my twenties. There was a lot of trial and error. A lot of interacting with others. A lot of false starts. A lot of reflection on uniqueness, strengths, personality, ancestry, and passions. A lot of small acts of obedience, making things more and more clear.

After Deborah and I got married, we left the Dallas area to help start a church for unchurched people in Seattle. Four years later, we moved to Los Angeles to serve at a church where people could belong before they believed. Then in 2010, we moved to Austin (where only 13 percent of people attend church on Sundays) to be a part of Gateway, a church where you can "come as you are."

In my thirties, I gained even more clarity when writing my book Not Like Me, about my journey of discovering God's love for all people—even those with whom we disagree, dislike, or differ. In the book, I try to help people of faith love the way Jesus loves, and I share humorous stories to open hearts and minds.

I am nothing quite like Dr. King or Andy Kaufman, but I have found my own voice.

I am called by God to advocate for the rights of those who don't yet believe!

I want to create space for people to share their struggles and doubts about God.

I want to help people to discover the God who created them and loves them and has a purpose for their life.

I want to help people, no matter where they are in their spiritual journey, discover a life-changing relationship with Jesus.

I want to catalyze community so that people from diverse

backgrounds can experience the love of God and find their calling.

Every follower of Jesus can find their purpose in loving God and loving others. As we step into loving God and loving others, the more specific purposes for our life become clearer and clearer.

Victor Frankl wrote the following in *Man's Search for Meaning*:

"For the meaning of life differs from man to man, from day to day and from hour to hour. What matters, therefore, is not the meaning of life in general but rather the specific meaning of a person's life at a given moment....

One should not search for an abstract meaning of life. Everyone has his own specific vocation or mission in life to carry out a concrete assignment which demands fulfillment. Therein he cannot be replaced, nor can his life be repeated. Thus, everyone's task is as unique as is his specific opportunity to implement it. As each situation in life represents a challenge to man and presents a problem for him to solve, the question of the meaning of life may be reversed.

Ultimately, man should not ask what the meaning of his life is, but rather he must recognize that it is he who is asked. In a word, each man is questioned by life; and he can only answer to life by answering for his own life; to life he can only respond by being responsible."

As we serve God and serve others, we find our calling.

Doing the right thing no matter how small it is...

Responding to the still, small voice inviting you to do something selfless and courageous...

Pursuing God and trusting His voice...

Believing Jesus, that if you lose your life in serving others, you will find your life.

Finding your calling is just as beautiful as the journey to discovering it, because along the way we experience the beauty of loving God and loving others.

A Life Worthy of Our Calling

When we feel like giving up, we need to remember our calling and live a life worthy of that calling. God can help us do this. Courage is earned when we overcome.

We need you to prevail to show us how you did it!

We can learn a valuable lesson from the Thessalonians, who suffered greatly. They faced violence, persecution, and riots because of their faith. They expected Jesus to return so soon that they stopped working. When a fake letter convinced them that Jesus had returned and did not come for them, they were disappointed and disillusioned.

Paul wrote to his friends and acknowledged the challenges they faced:

> You welcomed the message in the midst of severe suffering with the joy given by the Holy Spirit. And so you became a model to all the believers. . . your faith in God has become known everywhere. . . . " (I Thessalonians 1:6-8, NIV)

> Therefore, among God's churches we boast about your perseverance and faith in all the persecutions and trials you are enduring. (2 Thessalonians 1:4, NIV)

What God is calling you to do is worth the struggle, challenge, and hardship.

Paul acknowledged how difficult life had been for his friends in Thessalonika, but then he encouraged them: Don't give up!

For you know that we dealt with each of you as a father deals
with his own children, encouraging, comforting and urging
you to live lives worthy of God, who calls you into his kingdom
and glory. (1 Thessalonians 2:11-12, NIV)

We see this idea over and over in the Scriptures. When
things get tough, live a life worthy of the calling you've received.

With this in mind, we constantly pray for you, that our God
may make you worthy of his calling, and that by his power he
may bring to fruition your every desire for goodness and
your every deed prompted by faith. (2 Thessalonians
1:11, NIV)

Paul faced many difficulties of his own as he suffered
persecution, beatings, threats on his life, and imprisonment. In
other places, Paul wrote:

Now to him who is able to do immeasurably more than all we
ask or imagine, according to his power that is at work within
us, to him be glory in the church and in Christ Jesus
throughout all generations, for ever and ever! Amen. As a
prisoner for the Lord, then, I urge you to live a life worthy of
the calling you have received. Be completely humble and
gentle; be patient, bearing with one another in love. Make
every effort to keep the unity of the Spirit through the bond of
peace. (Ephesians 3:20-4:3, NIV)

Go back and reread these words as if they were written to
you by someone who believes God has great things in store
for you.

Not sure what to do? Just continue to do good.

So then, those who suffer according to God's will should commit themselves to their faithful Creator and continue to do good. (1 Peter 4:19, NIV)

Faithfulness means doing the right thing, no matter how small it is. Too often we give up too soon. We give up right before the breakthrough.

Consider what Harvard business professor Rosabeth Moss Kanter has said: "Everything looks like failure in the middle."

Some of us have spent too much time blaming our circumstances and blaming the environment. We need to remember who we are, remember Whose we are, and live a life worthy of the calling we have received.

Erwin McManus said: "The things we want God to do in our life demand that God sends us through a gauntlet that prepares us for that. We want God to use us in great ways, but we don't want God to prepare us for greatness."

His words remind me of what the British pastor and theologian Charles Spurgeon once said: "God gets His best soldiers out of the highlands of affliction."

To live a life worth of the calling we have received, we need to remain faithful to God even in the small things and rely on His help in our relationship with Him.

Small Successes

Consider for a moment: What is the trajectory of your life? Are you headed in the best direction? Are you in a better place now than you were a year ago at this time? If not, what are you going to do differently to make sure you make progress?

Sometimes we give up too soon because we cannot see the progress we are making. We are frustrated by comparing ourselves with others or even with who we want to be rather than realizing how far we have come. We need to be willing to make the right choices, no matter how small they are and no matter how long it takes.

Bill Gates once said, "We overestimate what we can accomplish in one year, but we underestimate what we can accomplish in ten years."

Some of us have way more cynicism and skepticism about genuine and lasting change. We've seen it over and over in our lives. We never seem to get traction. We expect we will be disappointed and become even more disillusioned if we try to make progress, so we just give up instead.

Here's one thing I know for sure: When we make only superficial changes, we won't see anything new. Instead, what we need is a complete overhaul. We need a new mind, and we need a new heart.

Jesus said that the greatest commandment is to love the Lord our God with all our heart, with all our soul, with all our mind, and with all our strength. These four categories cover all of who we are. Some of us are holding back one or two or three or all four of these from God. Over our entire lives, we will continue to fail to become all that God has created us to be until we completely give Him all of who we are.

Too often we attempt to change our behavior or change our circumstances. We just think, *If I had a new job, a new car, a new life group, a new relationship, a new. . . then I will finally find happiness.*

Rather than only trying to change our circumstances, we need to first allow God to help us better handle our circumstances.

There's a fascinating figure in the Scriptures named Hezekiah who gives us insight into a new life after overcoming trials. In his time, the kingdom of Israel had been divided into two nations, and then the Northern kingdom fell to Assyria. Judah in the South was barely hanging on. God continued to call the people back to Himself. They would make progress and then fall back again. This happened over and over. It was during this time that Hezekiah became king of Judah at the age of twenty-five. He ruled for twenty-nine years. Hezekiah's father was wicked and followed the ways of the wicked people around their nation—worshiping their gods, which included a brutal practice of sacrificing their children.

Hezekiah was different. He began removing all the items used to worship the false gods and abolished the practice of child sacrifice. 2 Chronicles 29 says the following:

> In the first month of the first year of his reign, he opened the doors of the temple of the Lord and repaired them. He brought in the priests and the Levites, assembled them in the square on the east side and said: "Listen to me, Levites! Consecrate yourselves now and consecrate the temple of the Lord, the God of your ancestors. Remove all defilement from the sanctuary. Our parents were unfaithful; they did evil in the eyes of the Lord our God and forsook him. . . . Now I intend to make a covenant with the Lord, the God of Israel, so that his fierce anger will turn away from us. My sons, do not be negligent now, for the Lord has chosen you to stand before him and serve him, to minister before him. . . ." (2 Chronicles 29:3-10, NIV)

As soon as he had the opportunity (in the first month of his first year), he changed the trajectory of his life and his nation from where his father had been going.

A Covenant with God

Often, we make New Year's resolutions and hope this will bring us lasting change. Typically, these changes last for a few weeks or a few days before we give up. Rather than making resolutions at the beginning of a new year, we need to make a covenant with God to experience a long-lasting transformation.

A covenant means fully trusting God with your whole heart, soul, mind, and strength. A covenant is more than believing in God or believing things about God. A covenant means having an intimate relationship with God in which He is allowed to inform all our decisions.

The best example of a covenant with God is marriage. Just like the healthiest marriages, a healthy relationship with God includes the following elements:

- Spending time together.
- Talking. (Praying.)
- Listening. (Reading the Scriptures and learning to keep in step with His Spirit.)
- Changing your behavior. (Adjusting what we like to what God likes.)
- Talking with others about your relationship. (Wearing a wedding ring shows the world that I am taken. Similarly, we need to learn how to share about our relationship with God in natural ways with others.)

Following Hezekiah's leadership, the people began to return to God and trust God in every aspect of life. Even with their finances and what they produced from their farms or when hunting, they began to give offerings to God, which were then distributed to those in need, so the community had plenty and abundance because of their willingness to personally sacrifice. What soon followed was a spiritual awakening. Amazing things were happening because Hezekiah made a choice to change the trajectory of his life.

Redefine Success

In this story is a really remarkable phrase describing Hezekiah, which gives us our second way to make our future better than our past:

> Hezekiah trusted in the Lord, the God of Israel. There was no one like him among all the kings of Judah, either before him or after him. He held fast to the Lord and did not stop following him; he kept the commands the Lord had given Moses. And the Lord was with him; he was successful in whatever he undertook. (2 Kings 18:5-7, NIV)

Now that sounds like the kind of person we want to be! How amazing would it be if when describing your life in a book they wrote about you:

"He was successful in whatever he tried"
"She was successful in whatever she tried"

If we stopped there, we would end up disappointed quite quickly in God if we thought, *If I just promise God I will do better, then he will give me success.* We should aspire toward a life described as successful in all that we do, but we must remember what success in the Scriptures really means.

We think of success as the opposite of failure or the absence of hardship. We define success in the dictionary as "the attainment of wealth, position, honors, or the like."

The Hebrew word used to describe Hezekiah means "to be prudent, be circumspect, wisely understand, prosper."

Success in the Scriptures means making wise choices, regardless of circumstances and over the long haul.

Hezekiah made wise choices no matter what he undertook. Wisdom is not some magical way of knowing the future.

Wisdom is the ability to connect cause and effect. Hezekiah understood that when he made his relationship with God his priority, everything else would come together.

Remove the Obstacles

When we are trying to make progress, we can hit an obstacle and give up. When we remove those things from our life, we can focus on God, which means keeping Him at the forefront of our mind through prayer and allowing Him to guide us throughout our day through prayer.

Hezekiah removed the things from his life and from his nation that were pointing toward false gods. He removed the things that distracted them from the One True God. The result was spiritual awakening!

So, if Hezekiah was successful in all that he did, then everything went well for him, right? Not at all. Hezekiah faced some tremendous challenges in his life. Two of those moments were shared multiple times in the Bible (2 Kings 18, 2 Chronicles 29, and Isaiah 36). In fact, Hezekiah had two moments in his life when his prayers created a new future!

Like so much of what we imagine in science fiction, Hezekiah was able to create a better alternative reality because of his relationship with God.

The Assyrians came back to do damage to Judah, just as they had done to Israel and to the neighboring Samaritans. Hezekiah had been able to buy time in the past from the Assyrians the last time they attacked. The Assyrians had never been defeated, and the field commander reminded the people of Judah of this. He shouted out threats. He promised destruction and tried to entice Hezekiah's top men to betray him. He shouted so that all the people of Judah could hear:

"Do not listen to Hezekiah. This is what the king of Assyria says: Make peace with me and come out to me. . . . Choose life and not death! Do not listen to Hezekiah, for he is misleading you when he says, 'The Lord will deliver us.'" (2 Kings 18:31-32, NIV)

The field commander for the Assyrians shouted out in the language of the people: Don't trust other nations to help you, don't trust your king, and don't trust your God. Even more confusing, the field commander even went on to claim: "'The Lord himself told me to march against this country and destroy it.'" (2 Kings 18:25, NIV)

You can imagine how tempting that would be. Who should you believe? Your king and the Assyrians both claimed God told them to do things that contradicted each other. Plus, the Assyrians had never lost!

Just like the people of Israel, we have voices trying to lead us in very different directions.

The people remained quiet, and Hezekiah turned to the Lord for help. He had made a covenant with God. He had surrendered himself and his decisions to God. Now Hezekiah tore his robes and put on sackcloth (a sign of desperation to God and to those who saw him). He went to the temple, and he prayed. The end of his prayer included this line:

"Now, Lord our God, deliver us from his hand, so that all the kingdoms of the earth may know that you, Lord, are the only God." (Isaiah 37:20, NIV)

Hezekiah had come to the place where he asked God to answer his prayer, not just to help him, and not even just to help his people, but to help others he didn't know.

Sometimes our prayers aren't answered because we aren't

desperate enough. Other times, our prayers aren't answered because they are too self-centered. Instead, we need to seek God with desperation and in a selfless way.

After this desperate and selfless prayer, God responded in a most amazing way:

> "Because you have prayed to me. . . . Have you not heard? Long ago I ordained it. In days of old I planned it; now I have brought it to pass." (Isaiah 37:26, NIV)

Now this is a bit mind-bending, but this is a moment in the Bible when God's sovereignty (His plan) interacts in a dynamic way with man's free will (our actions). The passage seems to be saying: "God had planned to stop the violence of the Assyrians in the future. It has already been planned. It is going to happen, but because of Hezekiah's prayer, God fast-forwarded into the future. Their violence against Judah would end now because of Hezekiah's prayer."

It is possible God's plan can be altered by our prayers and our behavior. God's overriding plan will happen, yet there is freedom and flexibility over the details of His plan.

At another moment in the Bible, God made this statement:

> "And if I announce that a nation or kingdom is to be built up and planted, and if it does evil in my sight and does not obey me, then I will reconsider the good I had intended to do for it." (Jeremiah 18:9-10, NIV)

It is possible for us to miss the good things God has intended for us when we choose to go our own way or give up too soon.

So Hezekiah, the man who was successful in everything that he did, still faced oppression from the Assyrians, threats from the Assyrians and others, and many other hardships. After he avoided certain destruction through his prayers, it wasn't too long later that he found himself in another precarious situation. Hezekiah suffered from an illness threatening to kill him. Once again he turned to God with a desperate prayer.

God's response: "'I have heard your prayer and seen your tears. I will add fifteen years to your life, and I will deliver you and this city from the hand of the king of Assyria. I will defend this city'" (Isaiah 38:5-6, NIV).

Remarkable! Hezekiah's choice to reach out to God once again altered God's plan for his life. He received fifteen more years! God's overriding plan remained in place, but there was room for Hezekiah to have fifteen more years on earth!

Even making wise choices, Hezekiah still faced tragedy and hardships. For example, during the time of his illness, Hezekiah failed to seek God's counsel on a decision that ended up putting his kingdom at risk from a new threat: the Babylonians. He was not perfect, and he failed to walk in wisdom 100 percent of the time. Even still, the man who was "successful at whatever he did" changed everything by making a covenant with God. He redefined success. His life was completely different than his father's life and even his son's life.

Each one of us must choose for ourselves the kind of life we want to live. Whether our parents were evil or whether they were living the right way, we still must make our own choices. We may face consequences for the choices our parents make, but we are not condemned by their bad choices, nor are we guaranteed good things by their good choices. We must choose our own adventure. We must choose if we will follow God and His ways or if we will reject Him and His ways.

Every day is another opportunity to make progress. We may be tempted to give up, but when we remember who we are, remember Whose we are, remember our calling, and redefine success, we can become tenacious.

Reflection:

When have you allowed a trial in your life to draw you closer to God?

When have you allowed a trial in your life to pull you away from Him and others?

Are you willing to ask God for help, forgiveness, and guidance on how to move forward, no matter what you may be facing?

Work through the section on "Trials" in Appendix A.

BECOMING INTENTIONAL:
OVERCOMING TEMPTATIONS

> Other seed fell among thorns, which grew up and choked the
> plants.... The seed falling among the thorns refers to someone
> who hears the word, but the worries of this life and the
> deceitfulness of wealth choke the word, making it unfruitful.
> (Matthew 13:7,22, NIV)

A Thorny Situation

MANY OF US fail to live up to our calling because we fall into the
temptations that seem to so easily distract or derail us.

Do you find yourself at times feeling overwhelmed with life?
Feeling choked by the thorns and distractions around you? Are
you derailed by anxiety or the pursuit of wealth?

Or do you get distracted while pursuing good things? As
Rick Shurtz, former Grow Pastor at Gateway Church in Austin,
says, "Sometimes we can turn what God intended as a gift to us
into our gods."

You meant well at first, but has providing for your family
now taken you away from your family? Or maybe you keep
going back to the same struggles over and over? Maybe you are
battling a generational sin or addiction that keeps you from

making progress. Maybe you don't even see how the choices you continue to make have been keeping you from God's better future for your life.

What keeps you from trusting God and following His path for your life? The third soil describes ground filled with thorns that grow up and choke anything good that grows. These thorns take the form of worries and the pursuit of wealth.

When we develop intentionality, we can overcome the temptations that distract us. We can move from being distracted toward experiencing clarity in our lives. Consumerism, depression, discontent, and pursuit of pleasure at all costs derail followers of Christ. When we simplify our lives and focus, we thrive despite the distractions around us.

Some of us are committed to so many different things, that we aren't really committed to any one thing. We have so many responsibilities at work and at home that we don't take care of either of them well. We are in and out of relationships, in and out of jobs, in and out of churches.

So how can we do this? How do we simplify?

Is it even possible to clear out a path and make progress?

The answer quite simply is: Yes! But it takes effort and intentionality. We can overcome temptations by becoming intentional.

The Scriptures give us the process to do just that. A pattern emerges throughout Paul's letters. It's a process right there in the Scriptures that has been passed down from generation to generation.

My life was completely transformed by applying these principles to my life. Here's the quick overview:

- Change your mind
- Change your actions
- Choose gratitude
- Commit to a healthy community

Choose a Growth Mindset

Some of us are growing and excited about our spiritual journey. We know we've made progress, and we realize we still have a lot to learn. Even still, if we are honest, some of us have hit a ceiling in our spiritual growth.

There are three reasons I think we stop growing.

1. Some of us don't believe we can grow. Too often, we come to closure too soon on who God is in our life or what we think God wants to do in our life. We don't believe God can do the miraculous. We've become cynical or jaded because of painful moments and what seem like unanswered prayers.

2. Some of us don't want to grow because it means change or making sacrifices. As a result, we settle for the status quo. We look back with fondness on the past, but we end up missing what God wants to do in us and through us right now and in the future!

3. Some of us feel like we want to grow, but we seem stuck. Some of that could be because we think we are more mature than we are. We confuse progress with maturity. We see the progress we have made, and we are satisfied with where we are now, especially as we compare ourselves to others. Unfortunately, this judgmental trap is what keeps us stuck. Let me just say this to be clear: none of us have arrived! I know I haven't.

Wherever you might be right now—growing, cynical about growing, settling, or stuck—the Scriptures tell us that "God is able to do more than we could ever ask or imagine" (Ephesians 3:20).

Sometimes we stop asking. Sometimes we stop imagining.

Sometimes we aren't asking for enough. Sometimes we aren't imagining enough.

What if you are settling for good, but what God has for you is *great*? What if you are settling for what comes naturally, but what God has for you is *supernatural*?

We are all imperfect people, which means we have not yet arrived at our full potential. How do we grow, and why do some people seem to stay stuck instead of growing?

Scientists point out that our mindset is critical to whether we will grow. The science of learning is backed by a basic understanding of neuroscience. In 1998, a study showed that the adult brain is capable of growing new brain cells. For many decades, it was thought that the brain was a "nonrenewable organ," that brain cells are bestowed in a finite amount and slowly die as we age, whether we attempt to keep them around or not. But we've learned that if our brains are functioning properly, we can always learn, improve existing capabilities, and develop new skills. Our brains can grow as we age.

In her book *Mindset: The New Psychology of Success*, Dr. Carol Dweck points out the differences between a fixed mindset vs. a growth mindset. She writes how some of us have a "fixed mindset" that makes us fearful of being judged by God or others, so we play the game of putting on a good face to feel loved or valued—but that keeps us stuck. We believe things like the following:

- "Failure is the limit of my abilities."
- "I'm either good at it or I'm not."
- "My abilities are unchanging."
- "I stick to what I know."
- "Feedback and criticism are personal."

Dr. Dweck contends that we need to have a "growth-mindset" so that we can see our failures and shortcomings, but in the light of grace. We must see them as opportunities to learn and grow and keep moving toward a better version of ourselves. We must embrace the fact that we are imperfect people with room to grow! (Maybe that's what has drawn so many people to our church, Gateway, where we say, "No perfect people are allowed.") People with a growth mindset believe things like the following:

- "Failure is an opportunity to grow."
- "My effort and my attitude determine my abilities."
- "Feedback is constructive."
- "I'm inspired by the success of others."
- "I like to try new things."

This all reminds me of Martin Seligman's book *Learned Optimism*, where he writes that "pessimistic people think of setbacks as *permanent, universal, and internal*; but optimistic people see setbacks as *temporary, specific, and external*."

From a Cretan to an Overseer

Science often proves what the Scriptures have said all along. The Bible has made this distinction between a fixed mindset and a growth mindset for thousands of years before science discovered this idea.

One of the most influential people to ever live was a man named Paul. He traveled all across the Middle East and what is now Europe, reaching out to people and starting churches. He always traveled with others, and he often left those he mentored to lead the churches he helped start. He then wrote letters to the churches he started and the church leaders he mentored. These letters make up most of the New Testament and have shaped followers of Jesus and our world! He took the words of Jesus and applied them in the context of community. The churches he started spread all over the known world and have continued to spread to this day.

In one situation, Paul left Titus in Crete, an island just south of Greece. Titus' goal was described as the following:

> The reason I left you in Crete was that you might put in order what was left unfinished and appoint elders in every town, as I directed you. (Titus 1:5, NIV)

Paul goes on to describe elders as spiritual overseers who have integrity. They aren't corrupt or given to stealing or drunkenness. Instead, they are slow to anger, trustworthy, hospitable, and demonstrate self-control. They are faithful to their spouses, and they know and live out the truths found in the Scriptures. In essence, they are spiritually mature.

Paul points out to Titus that he realizes what a difficult task this is, because there weren't a lot of people in Crete that matched that description. You see, the Cretans had a fixed mindset.

One of Crete's own prophets has said it: "Cretans are always liars, evil brutes, lazy gluttons." (Titus 1:12, NIV)

Think about this for a second! The Cretans all believed this about themselves:

- "We are always lying."
- "We are all evil brutes."
- "We are all lazy gluttons."

In other words, "This is just who are. There is no changing us. There is no hope for us. If you don't like the way we are, then go to another island."

Even to this day, to refer to someone as a "cretin" is not a compliment.

Can you imagine how Titus must have felt? Titus' goal was

to create a community in which evil people became overseers, a community where unlikeable people became world-class leaders. Titus' job was to turn people who had a fixed mindset into people with a growth mindset. Paul left him there basically saying: "Titus, I want you to turn Cretans, people who are always liars, evil brutes, and gluttons into spiritual overseers."

Now I want to show you one of the funniest lines in the entire Bible. After quoting the rude description of Cretans from their own prophet, Paul wrote:

This saying is true. (Titus 1:13, NIV)

I cannot help but think Paul was joking with his young friend Titus, because throughout the rest of the letter Paul shows him how to help them change and grow, to move from being lying, evil, lazy, and gluttonous brutes to becoming trustworthy, godly, and honorable spiritual leaders.

So then, what is the process Paul and his mentees used to help people become the people God created them to be? Paul emphasized winning the personal battle between the flesh and the Spirit, and that battle began in the mind. He also emphasized the importance of community. At the same time, we take personal responsibility for our spiritual growth, we also commit to live life in community, allowing others to help us as we help them. Together we bring light and life to the world around us. Through it all, transformation is motivated by gratitude for all God has given us.

Take Every Thought Captive to Renew Your Mind

To the Corinthians, a group of people really struggling to overcome the temptations of this world, Paul encourages them that the battle to change begins in the mind. He writes in 2 Corinthians 10:5, "We take captive every thought."

Paul is challenging the church not to bring the social stratifications and separations of society into the church. Paul believed that through Jesus, Jews and Gentiles were coming together to form new multiethnic communities where men, women, slave, and free all belonged. Paul wants the Corinthians to avoid living by the standards of the world. He is reminding them that we do not use the weapons or methods of the world. When he then says, "We take every thought captive," his primary point is that we make every "way of thinking" consistent with or obedient to the way of Christ. As this is a letter to a church, he is focused on the culture of the community. The individual then must be wary of what he or she is thinking and believing in order to stay in alignment with God's design for the community.

To do that, every thought that comes into our mind that distracts us or takes us down the wrong path needs to be taken captive.

A newer translation of the Bible called The Voice translates 2 Corinthians 10:5 like this: "We are taking prisoners of every thought, every emotion. . . ."

So often how we feel determines how we act. Instead, our actions can precede our emotions. No matter how emotionally driven you are, you've seen this work. We wake up and don't feel like working out. We do it anyway, and we feel so much better, and we're even glad that we did it.

If you struggle with letting your emotions control you, come up with a plan for what you know you should be doing, and get others to keep you accountable to help you in that. Then do what you know you should do, no matter how you feel about it later.

For others of us, it's our thoughts rather than our emotions that lead us astray. We come to closure too soon on an issue, or we judge others unfairly.

Our thoughts and emotions can lead us down the wrong path!

As mentioned previously, the thoughts we have that are from God include the following:

- Thoughts that compel us toward selflessness.
- Thoughts that require courage to pull them off.
- Thoughts that are consistent with God's character.

Unfortunately, we aren't as familiar with God's voice. Instead, we are quite familiar with thoughts that come from a dark place. As a result of the brokenness and pain in our lives and in this world, we find ourselves believing lies about ourselves, about others, and about our future. Unaware of the spiritual battle we face, there are other voices and forces opposing our progress.

What lies shape your life? What limitations have you imposed on your future based on negative input from others? What struggles have been passed down to you from your family tree?

For example, I grew up believing all Bryant men were easily angered and all Bryant women were anxious. I just assumed that would be how I would always be, and there was no real reason to try and change this. Believing like this abdicated my responsibility to mature and change and indicated a lack of faith that God could help me live differently. It was almost as if I believed my genetics were more powerful than God's Spirit.

I used to have a fixed mindset. My last name "Bryant" means "noble, strong, and virtuous," but I used to believe that "All Bryants are controlling, short-tempered, anxious, and cheap."

I had seen glimpses of Bryants being empowering, calm, peaceful, and generous—but they had all married into our family!

In the context of authentic community, I discovered I don't

have to be the controlling, angry, and anxious tightwad I had assumed I would always be.

Your family of origin does not have to limit you. Your last name does not have to define you.

As you seek God and become intentional about growing in your faith in community, you can become the person God created you to be. Your family needs you to make growing spiritually a priority. Your neighborhood, your workplace, and your friends all need you to make growing spiritually a priority.

Don't Eat MORE FOOD!

In 2009 I was working on my dissertation as I was finishing up my doctorate. I had stopped exercising, and I wasn't really eating healthy either. I was sitting at the computer all day working on this project, and I kept thinking that I needed to make some healthier choices, but I never got around to doing so. I was putting it off until the project was completed.

One day, my back was hurting at the end of a long day at the computer. I told my wife that I really needed to lose some weight or else my back might go out. Even still, I kept putting it off.

Our minds are powerful things. I remember thinking to myself, *Don't eat more food! Don't eat more food!*

Unfortunately, the last two words in my mind echoed: "More food! More food!" As a result, I found myself eating more food.

Eventually on the last day of 2009, I woke up in the worst pain of my entire life. A disc in my back had ruptured. I was experiencing what's called sciatica, which is the firing of nerves down my leg into my foot. It was so painful that as we went to the ER I was barely able to remain conscious! They sent me home with pain medication hoping it would resolve on its own. It did not. Finally, I had back surgery, after waiting for a month, followed by another seven weeks of recovering.

I didn't have time to do what I knew was right, so in the end I had three months off to regret not doing what I knew I should have done. I ate so much I had to have back surgery! What I've learned in the process is that I shouldn't just think about what I do not want to do, but I should start taking every thought captive and start thinking about what I want to do. Now, whenever that temptation to have that fourth meal comes right around 9:00 p.m. at night, I drink water instead. I started chewing gum when I wanted a snack. I removed the peanut M&M's from my office.

Our minds are powerful and can hold us hostage where we are. Taking our thoughts captive allows us the opportunity to renew our minds.

Here's how this can work: A common struggle for me has been anxiety. I find I do really well in the midst of a real crisis, but I tend to struggle more over anticipated crises. When something really goes wrong, I often know the best moves to make, but when I am afraid of things going wrong, I am unproductive and can become a wreck!

In my mind I think, *Don't worry. Don't worry.* And in the end, the last thing in my mind is, *Worry. Worry.* Suddenly, I am worrying about worrying!

Once again, the Bible has a path out that includes taking our thoughts captive and renewing our minds.

> Do not be anxious about anything, but in every situation, by prayer and petition, with thanksgiving, present your requests to God. And the peace of God, which transcends all understanding, will guard your hearts and your minds in Christ Jesus. 8 Finally, brothers and sisters, whatever is true, whatever is noble, whatever is right, whatever is pure, whatever is lovely, whatever is admirable—if anything is excellent or praiseworthy—think about such things. (Philippians 4:6-8, NIV)

When you find yourself stuck worrying and fighting anxiety

and fear, stop. Start praying by thanking God. Notice it doesn't just say, "Present your petitions to God." Paul knew we could get caught just praying very anxious prayers. Rather than our time in prayer just being all about what we need or what we want, we need to take the time to acknowledge all He has already done for us!

Consider your thoughts: Are they taking you in a positive direction or in a negative one? If negative, then take that thought captive and renew your mind by going down a different path.

Measure your thoughts by the words Paul uses. Are your thoughts pure, praiseworthy, lovely, admirable, noble, true, excellent, or right? If not, then you are going in the wrong direction. Consider this acronym to help you remember what to think about to take your mind in a positive direction. Think about the only those things which are the following:

- Pure
- Praiseworthy
- Lovely
- Admirable
- Noble
- True
- Excellent
- Right

The acronym spells "planter" with two "p"s. Like a planter, our mind reaps what we sow. If you sow dark thoughts, you will reap dark actions. Sometimes we cannot get scary or anxious thoughts out of our heads because we won't stop putting them in there! If you sow God-honoring thoughts, your actions will follow.

Take Off the Old to Put on the New

Over and over, Paul writes to church after church, in city after city, something very different than what those of us who grew up going to church might have heard.

I grew up in church hearing all about what we needed to stop doing. I saw Christianity as a giant "Don't Do List." The problem is that I never understood why we should avoid these behaviors. What I didn't hear was that this was a list of things that hurt us and brought pain into our lives and the lives of others. For the longest time, I never realized God was offering a better alternative. God's message to us is, "Come as You Are, and You Don't Have to Stay That Way!"

There is so much hope and beauty in that!

To the Ephesians, Paul wrote:

. . . . put off your old self, which is being corrupted by its deceitful desires; to be made new in the attitude of your minds; and to put on the new self, created to be like God in true righteousness and holiness. (Ephesians 4:22-24, NIV)

To the Galatians, Paul wrote to take off the "sinful nature" and put on the "fruit of the Spirit."

To the Colossians, Paul wrote:

You have taken off your old self with its practices and have put on the new self, which is being renewed in knowledge in the image of its Creator. (Colossians 3:9-10, NIV)

When we choose to follow Christ, let Him lead us, and follow His ways, we do not have to live the same way anymore!

Let's get practical for a moment. Consider an area of your life in which you struggle. Maybe you find yourself making the same New Year's resolution year after year. Do you have an issue in your mind? Not sure? Then ask someone who knows you well: "What is my issue?" If they know you and love you enough to be honest, they probably know!

Maybe your issue is greed. Instead of never being satisfied and demanding more from others, we can become generous.

> Anyone who has been stealing must steal no longer, but must work, doing something useful with their own hands, that they may have something to share with those in need. (Ephesians 4:28, NIV)

Do you see the progression? Stop taking from others. Instead work so you can not only care for yourself but so that you can care for others.

Some of us aren't moving forward in becoming who God wants us to be because we struggle with an issue that keeps us stuck. Maybe your struggle with lust, anxiety, anger, foolishness, lack of self-control, or some other struggle is why you have stopped making progress. God may be protecting you from more because He knows your character cannot handle more quite yet. Here's the great news: There is a pathway out!

Whatever struggle you came up with as your issue: Look it up in the Bible *and* look up the antidote. Focus on "putting on the new." That's how we take off the old!

Eliminate Bad Habits to Start Good Habits

This process gets easier as we learn to connect cause and effect. We need to realize that when we dive into the deep end of the pool of darkness, we are going to get wet.

Go backwards. Figure out the triggers that lead to the behavior you want to overcome and eliminate those. It may be something as simple as driving a new route home from work to avoid driving by the house of the guy where you bought weed, taking the Instagram app off your phone for a season to avoid getting sucked into hours online, or going to bed at 10:00 p.m. so you avoid going online to places you don't want to go.

In Los Angeles, a young friend of mine struggled with connecting with others and even with depression. One day I was checking on how he was doing, and he said, "I don't feel connected at our church."

So, I asked him, "When is the last time you came on a Sunday?"

His response: "Six weeks ago."

I had an incredible insight in that moment for him. So, I told him, "You feel disconnected because you are disconnected." Profound, huh? He felt discouraged because he had removed himself from people who would encourage him.

I tried to help him see that his choice to stay away was one of the reasons why he felt disconnected. Sundays are more than just a message and music. He could listen to the music on Spotify and the message online. I encouraged him that the Bible encourages us not to give up meeting together but to meet up regularly so we can connect with God *and* connect with others.

When we come late and leave early, we are missing opportunities to connect with God and connect with others, but if we come early, fully engage, and stay late, we maximize our opportunities! To fully engage means to come asking God to show you what He has for you, and to show you what He wants from you. He may speak to you through the music, the message, or a conversation after the service, and He may lead you to meet a specific need as you look for ways to serve others and serve Him.

How do we overcome the evil that so entangles us? Paul gives us a clue as he describes the role of spiritual leaders, those considered apostles, prophets, evangelists, pastors, and teachers. Paul challenged the Ephesian leaders in Ephesus with the following:

To prepare God's people for works of service, so that the body of Christ may be built up until we all reach unity in the faith and knowledge of the Son of God and become mature, attaining to the whole measure of the fullness of Christ. (Ephesians 4:12-13, NIV)

Serving leads to maturity. When we fail to serve, we hijack from ourselves an opportunity to grow. We need to serve more than others need our help. When we lose our lives in serving, that is how we find our lives.

Often, we make progress only to fall again. During this relapse, we give up trying. Remember: Messing up does not have to mean giving up! Get right back up and start over. The more we succeed, the more confident we will become. Furthermore, it is not a sin to be tempted. Just because a thought comes crashing into your mind does not mean you have to act on it. Just having the thought can derail us or discourage us unless we put these principles into practice. Therefore, it is so important to take every thought captive and renew your mind.

Here's what's amazing: When we choose to follow Jesus, the Spirit of God comes to live within us, and we have access to the mind of Christ (1 Corinthians 2:9-16)!

It's important to realize that Jesus can relate to us. He knows our pain and struggle.

For we do not have a high priest who is unable to empathize with our weaknesses, but we have one who has been tempted in every way, just as we are—yet he did not sin. (Hebrews 4:15, NIV)

The same power that helped Him say "no" is within us.

His divine power has given us everything we need to experience life and to reflect God's true nature through the

90

knowledge of the One who called us by His glory and virtue. (2 Peter 1:3, The Voice)

From the moment we are born spiritually, we have everything we need to be spiritually mature. We see this in babies. Healthy babies have ten fingers and ten toes and two arms and two legs. Babies would not be nearly as cute if they came out with just a head at birth and then a few months later a torso popped out, followed later by legs and arms, and then finally fingers and toes.

No, we are born with everything we need to be fully mature adults. We are just smaller and need time to mature. We have everything we need to become who we were created to be.

In Ephesians 1:19-20, Paul goes on to say that we have access to the same power that rose Christ from the dead!

We need to rely on God's help and the encouragement of others, but we can do this. We don't have to stay this way!

Still struggling to get started? If so, choose to move forward for others and with help from others. I think of my uncle who quit smoking the day his first child was born. He couldn't quit on his own, but he could quit for his son.

If you aren't willing to take care of yourself now, then you won't be able to take care of others later.

Let your motivation come from a deeply spiritual place—out of gratitude to God.

We are saved by grace through faith (Ephesians 2:8-9), and we need to live by grace through faith (Colossians 2:6-7). God's part in becoming who we were created to be is his grace: the love He lavishes on us even though we don't deserve it. When it comes to our part (and He helps us even with this), gratitude compels us.

Commit to a Healthy Community

Paul was going to all sorts of crazy places with very broken people who had no understanding of a loving and just God or who believed in lots of gods.

What was the process? The process was relational. They started a church. The early church met all together in large gatherings and in homes—just like we do. Paul describes all of these in this statement in Acts:

> I served the Lord with great humility and with tears and in the midst of severe testing.... You know that I have not hesitated to preach anything that would be helpful to you but have taught you publicly and from house to house. I have declared to both Jews and Greeks that they must turn to God in repentance and have faith in our Lord Jesus. (Acts 20:19-21, NIV)

Paul was accepting of people no matter their background. He grew up as a very strict Jew, but he was now accepting of what he was told were unclean people to avoid, including anyone who was not Jewish, Greeks, and what he called "Gentiles." He was serving with humility and helping people grow as they gathered publicly and in homes. He was helping people find faith.

Discipleship is relational. We cannot grow to overcome temptations that currently distract us without others in our lives. We cannot reach our full potential on our own. We need people to love us, encourage us, rebuke us, challenge us, and be with us on this journey. We need community to become all who God created us to be. We need to surround ourselves with healthy people who have a growth mindset to learn how to have one ourselves.

Maybe you have heard this before from Jim Rohn: "We are the average of the five people we spend the most time with."

So, with whom are you spending time? Are you with people who live in a way you want to one day live your life? Are you inviting people into your life who are exploring faith or are new to faith to help them in their journey?

We were made for relationships, both with God and others. Authentic community is essential to developing personally and spiritually.

In my own life, I have been transformed in the context of healthy community. I have grown to overcome struggles in my life through meaningful conversations in the lobby of a church building or in someone's home, through the insights discovered in a message on Sunday or in a Bible study, through the encounters with God while singing with others, through the experiences serving others with others, and through the friends who listened to me, prayed with me, shared with me, encouraged me, kept me accountable, and even corrected me.

It is important to remember that most of the books in the New Testament were written to churches. Following Jesus is not intended to be just between you and God. If it was then when we were baptized, the person baptizing us should have just held us under the water so we could go straight to heaven! Instead, they brought us out of the water because we have a purpose to fulfill on this side of eternity: We are to love God and love others.

You were meant for community—a community that helps you live God's way rather than get sucked into the destructive ways of the world.

We Need Each Other

Another passage that helped me switch my mindset was the book of Hebrews. This book was a sermon written to a group of Jewish Christians who were suffering under tremendous persecution. Some of those in the church had given up on their faith in Jesus. The author of Hebrews reminds them that Jesus was the fulfillment of the Hebrew Scriptures. Jesus was the ultimate sacrifice, dying on the cross for our sins, so there is no need to sacrifice animals for forgiveness. Jesus came as the ultimate Priest, Prophet, and King. He was and is greater than the angels and Moses. He was and is the promised Messiah.

In Hebrews 10, we read this encouragement:

> Let us hold tightly without wavering to the hope we affirm, for God can be trusted to keep his promise. Let us think of ways to motivate one another to acts of love and good works. And let us not neglect our meeting together, as some people do, but encourage one another, especially now that the day of his return is drawing near. (Hebrews 10:24-25, NIV)

We should not neglect coming together—on Sundays and in our homes as followers of Jesus have done since the Church began. Motivating one another to acts of love and good works happens best with others around you. Encouraging one another happens when we are with each other. We need each other!

We live isolated and lonely lives by default.

- An NPR report in 2019 indicated that three out of five Americans are lonely.
- A 2018 Cigna Study found that 47 percent of Americans said that they don't have meaningful in-person social interactions, such as an extended conversation with a friend or quality time with family on a daily basis, and the emerging Generation Z is the loneliest generation of them all—perhaps because of all the screen time.
- The Alameda County Study on Relationships found that loneliness can have the health effects of smoking fifteen cigarettes a day. . . and that loneliness can lead to an early death.

- In the book *The Search of The Common Good*, Jake Meador states that between 1940 and 2010 the population grew by 134 percent. During that same timeframe, the number of service and therapeutic professionals (like therapists, counselors, mental health professionals, psychologists, social workers, and so on) rose by 3,206 percent.
- Steven Marche wrote in *The Atlantic* that "We have outsourced the work of everyday caring."
- We've replaced having a few genuine friends with having hundreds of Facebook "friends" we really don't know, other than what they ate for lunch yesterday when they post pics of their meals.

This has only gotten even harder since the pandemic.

So ask yourself: who is spurring you on in life and in your faith? Also consider: Who are you spurring on?

This was so important to the author of Hebrews because too many were falling away from the community, which was the step taken before falling away from their faith. He goes on to say:

> You need to persevere so that when you have done the will of God, you will receive what he has promised. For, "In just a little while, he who is coming will come and will not delay." And, "But my righteous one will live by faith. And I take no pleasure in the one who shrinks back." But we do not belong to those who shrink back and are destroyed, but to those who have faith and are saved. (Hebrews 10:36-39, NIV)

I love this! Did you see the switch from a fixed mindset to a growth mindset?

The author of Hebrews is saying: "You may think of yourself as a quitter—someone who shrinks back and gives up—but with God's help you are not a quitter. That's not who you are! Jesus has changed your identity!"

When we say "yes" to following Jesus, when we ask God to forgive us and to lead us, we are made new. We are made righteous because of what Jesus did for us by dying on the cross for us. We are new with the Spirit of God within us! We have the same power that rose Jesus from the dead within us, and we are overcomers! We do not shrink back, because He helps us stand strong! God is pleased with us because He loves us, and He sees us through the righteousness of Jesus and what He did for us!

We are creating distance between ourselves and God when we give up. When we live with a fixed mindset, we are living life as if there were no God or that God cannot do more than we ever asked or imagined. When we shrink back or when we turn back from our faith because of fear, that is not who we are. God is not pleased when we shrink back, but (and this is a big *but*), we are not those who shrink back! We forget who we are! Unfortunately, we do this far too often.

Community reminds us of who we are and helps us live out the new version of ourselves that God created us to be.

Motivated By Grace

Later in the letter to Titus, Paul gives more insight into what should be happening in a healthy community. Paul and Titus started a church where people were close enough to others in their community to have honest and sometimes hard conversations. In chapter 2, to help the Cretans grow and even overcome their destructive habits and pursuits, Paul writes these words:

> For the grace of God has appeared that offers salvation to all
> people. It teaches us to say 'No' to ungodliness and worldly
> passions, and to live self-controlled, upright and godly lives in

this present age, while we wait for the blessed hope—the appearing of the glory of our great God and Savior, Jesus Christ, who gave himself for us to redeem us from all wickedness and to purify for himself a people that are his very own, eager to do what is good. (Titus 2:11-13, (NIV)

God's part in becoming who we were created to be is His grace—the love He lavishes on us even though we don't deserve it. God has given us so much. He has done so much for us! Our lives should be motivated by a deep sense of gratitude. We should passionately serve Him and follow Him, willing to say "no" to the temptations that come our way.

Our part (and He helps us even with this) is to live out this new life by saying "no" to the temptations of this world, out of gratitude. God's grace compels us to do the good we were created to do. We need to reflect on all the great things God has given us.

As Erwin McManus has said, "We need to be thankful for what we have and not mad about what we don't have."

Some of us grew up in a religious context, which inadvertently or intentionally may have taught us that we need to do good things to get God to love us. The God in the Scriptures is actually a God of grace, which means we are loved even though we don't deserve it. We do good out of gratitude for what God has done.

We need to shift our understanding of God and the Church. Christianity is not about religion but about a relationship with God.

Cultural Christianity and American religiosity is more of a fixed mindset about God, our heavenly Father, which says: "I messed up. My Father is going to kill me."

Genuine faith in Jesus and having a relationship with God is more of a growth mindset which says: "I messed up. I need to call my Dad."

How do you view your relationship with God? Is he always angry and unwilling to answer your prayers—so why even pray? Or do you see Him as loving and there with you in the midst of your most difficult moments?

Being in a healthy community helps us in this. Too often we slip back into a religious mindset (a fixed mindset) rather than a relational mindset (a growth mindset). Getting into a community where there's "no perfect people allowed" and where we value authenticity changes us—a place where we can be authentic, confessing our struggles, and experiencing healing as a community growing together.

James, the leader of the Jerusalem church, wrote:

> Therefore confess your sins to each other and pray for each other so that you may be healed. The prayer of a righteous person is powerful and effective. (James 5:16, NIV)

Dudley

I saw the power of gratitude back when I was a substitute teacher in Waco.

First, let me just say that substitute teachers do not get paid enough.

When I worked as a substitute teacher, I discovered that evil lurks in the hearts of children. I suppose I was just experiencing personally what I had inflicted on the subs who had to have me in their classroom. One of the first classes that I taught as a substitute was a second-grade class. I began the day smiling and encouraging the children. Soon they turned on me. A pencil sword fight broke out in one corner of the room as a few other kids started running around the classroom. Those not fighting or running were yelling at each other. As I tried to stop the kids from running and to quiet the rest of the classroom, a girl approached me with tears streaming down her face and *a pencil sticking out of her hand.* Apparently, she had lost the pencil sword fight. Somehow, I made it through that chaotic day. I learned a valuable lesson that day: Substitute teachers should never smile.

My next assignment was a kindergarten class. These five-year-old kids were in for quite an experience. I was going to be so strict that they would pray for their regular teacher's quick return. As I was teaching them how to write the letter "D" (in upper and lower case), I had a scowl on my face. During my lesson I noticed a little guy named Dudley was crying. I approached him and asked why he was crying. He was unable to answer through his tears. The little guy next to him responded, "He doesn't know how to write his 'D's'." This was a problem. There was a capital "D" and a lower case "d" in his name!

I kneeled next to Dudley and began helping him form the letters on his paper. By holding his hand while he held the pencil, he slowly made progress as we wrote several "D's" and "d's" in between those gigantic lines on his paper. Soon he stopped crying. Later in the day, Dudley came running up to me and handed me a Valentine. It was a few days after the holiday. I read the Valentine, which was signed in cursive "Love, Jennifer." Confused for a moment, I then realized what he had done. To thank me for helping him learn to write his 'd's,' he wanted to give me the only gift he had to give: a used Valentine's Day card.

We need to reflect on all of the great things that God has given us. We have life, breath, health, family, friends, freedom, a new life in Christ, and so on. He has done so much for us and given so much to us! Our lives should be motivated by a deep sense of gratitude. We should passionately serve Him and follow Him willing to endure any trial that comes our way.

When we are compelled by gratitude to become the best version of ourselves, we experience something we deeply long for.

We need to stop trying to change by our own power. We need to surrender all to God and let Him help us become who we deeply long to become. We cannot do this on our own. We become the best version of ourselves amid community and support.

Reflection:

How does God want you to "take off the old" so you can "put on the new"?

From what does He want to free you?

Are you willing to ask God for help, forgiveness, and guidance on how to move forward, no matter what you may be facing?

Work through the section on "Temptations" in Appendix A.

BECOMING PROACTIVE:
OVERCOMING SELFISHNESS

After this, Jesus traveled about from one town and village to another, proclaiming the good news of the kingdom of God. The Twelve were with him, and also some women who had been cured. . . . These women were helping to support them out of their own means. While a large crowd was gathering and people were coming to Jesus from town after town, he told this parable. . . . "Still other seed fell on good soil. It came up and yielded a crop, a hundred times more than was sown. This is the meaning of the parable: But the seed on good soil stands for those with a noble and good heart, who hear the word, retain it, and by persevering produce a crop." (Luke 8:1-4,8,11,15, NIV)

THE FOURTH SOIL describes ground that produces fruit—a harvest a hundred times greater than what was planted. It is natural and normal for all who follow Christ to bear fruit—to be transformed and transforming others.

The natural result of following Jesus is a life described as fruitful, rich, and productive. If we can become receptive, tenacious, and intentional, we will find ourselves in a position to respond to do the right thing. Knowing the right thing to do is a tremendous challenge. Choosing to do the right thing is sometimes even tougher. We can become proactive, and, as a result, bear fruit.

Hearing God and following God requires proactivity and helps us overcome our tendency toward apathy, rebellion, or selfishness. We can move from a more desolate place toward a more creative, generative, productive, and fruitful one when we choose to live for others and die to self.

Obedience

The good soil describes someone who hears the word, understands it, and produces a crop. In other words, they obey. The words used to describe hearing, retaining, and understanding all imply action: obeying God. If you hear, you will respond. If you retain or put to memory what you hear, you will live it out. If you understand, you will do it. Jesus was saying, "If you comprehend my message, then you will put it into action. When you act on what you hear, you will bear fruit."

Even in our culture, we equate hearing with doing. When you were younger, did your parents ever ask you, "Are you listening to me?" Our parents equate listening with obeying. When our parents say, "You aren't being a good listener," this means, "you aren't doing what I am asking you to do." When our parents say, "Do you understand what I'm saying?" then they are really implying, "If you understand me, then you will trust what I am saying and act on it."

Unfortunately, we often rebel. We know what we ought to do, and don't do it. Or we know what we shouldn't do, and we do it anyway.

We treat God the same way we treated our parents when we were kids. Too often, we aren't good listeners.

To be proactive means we hear and act on what we hear. The key to overcoming rebellion is becoming proactive. Being proactive means doing what you know you ought to do and stop doing the things you know you shouldn't do.

Proactive means "acting in advance to deal with an expected difficulty; anticipatory." Synonyms include "aggressive," "ardent," "banzai," "can-do," "eager," "energetic," "enthused," "enthusiastic," "fanatical," "fired up," and "intense."

A proactive person doesn't remain a victim, no matter what they may face. A proactive person doesn't complain about something they are unwilling to do anything about!

While walking this earth, Jesus would often say things to scare away those who were not serious about making a commitment to him and to his leadership in their lives. He wanted to clarify that he was not simply on earth to offer a free medical clinic. He was ultimately here to do something more extraordinary than teach great truths, heal diseases, and raise the dead. He was here to perform the greatest miracle of all: to transform lives.

A Christ-follower follows Christ. We strive to become who He has created us to be by surrendering everything to Him, and He will give us back only what's best for us.

When we live the way of Christ, we obey Christ.

Throughout the Scriptures, we see a connection between listening to God and doing what He says.

> "Not everyone who says to me, 'Lord, Lord,' will enter the kingdom of heaven, but only the one who does the will of my Father who is in heaven." (Matthew 7:21, NIV)

Rather than saying "yes" with our mouths but living out "no" with our actions, a disciple listens to God and follows Him wherever He may lead.

> "Therefore everyone who hears these words of mine and puts them into practice is like a wise man who built his house on

the rock. . . . But everyone who hears these words of mine and does not put them into practice is like a foolish man who built his house on sand." (Matthew 7:24-26, NIV)

When our lives are built on the rock, we will last through the storms. When our lives are built on the sand, we won't.

Do not merely listen to the word, and so deceive yourselves. Do what it says. (James 1:22, NIV)

Only those who trust God obey Him.

Obedience has negative connotations in our society but think of obeying God as being invited by someone to your surprise party. You don't know why they are asking you to do what they are asking, but you know you can trust them. The result of obeying them (even though you don't want to) is a fantastic party (even if it wasn't totally a surprise).

God's Love Language

Are you familiar with the 5 Love Languages? The idea is that you express love either by giving gifts, giving words of affirmation, spending quality time, spending quantity time, doing acts of service, or physical touch. However you express love is also how you prefer to receive love.

When my wife and I were dating, I made her a mix tape as a Christmas gift which took lots of time and effort. She bought me a $200 gold necklace. I looked like Mr. T. from the A-Team! The next year she bought me a $300 suit! By this point we were engaged, so I felt I needed to share with Deborah that I don't like expensive gifts because soon she would be spending our money on things I didn't want. After sharing with her I would prefer something like a homemade meal than a suit I would rarely wear, she said: "I am so glad we are talking about this because you are a terrible gift giver!" We were missing each other because we were expressing love for each other in ways the other did not fully understand. I express love through acts of service whereas Deborah loves gifts.

When we trust God by obeying Him, we express our love to Him. God's love language is trust.

"Whoever has my commands and keeps them is the one who loves me." (John 14:21, NIV)

In fact, if you know the right thing to do and don't do it, that, for you, is evil. (James 4:17, MSG)

When it comes to trusting and obeying God, often we may struggle. Some of us get stuck because we don't know what to do. Others of us struggle because we don't want to do what we know we should do. Some of us struggle to stop doing what we know we shouldn't do.

In the Scriptures, Abraham was known as the one God chose to bless so that all nations would be blessed. Abraham had to trust God and follow God on a journey to the Promised Land for this blessing to take effect.

Consider the story of Abraham's dad, named Terah.

Terah took his son Abram, his grandson Lot son of Haran, and his daughter-in-law Sarai, the wife of his son Abram, and together they set out from Ur of the Chaldeans to go to Canaan. But when they came to Harran, they settled there. 32 Terah lived 205 years, and he died in Harran. (Genesis 11:31-32, NIV)

Sound like a familiar destination? Terah was on the way to the Promised Land, but he stopped halfway!

Terah, Abraham's father, was on his way to Canaan, later

known as the Promised Land, but he stopped in Harran and died there. Consider for a moment: What if he had made it all the way there? If Terah had not stopped, then Abraham would not have needed to leave his family to go to the Promised Land, because he would have already been there.

Is it possible God promised Terah the same thing he promised Abraham, but Terah stopped halfway there?

What if what you feel God has promised you is just around the corner?

Do not stop halfway! Don't give up now!

When God gives you an opportunity, seize it!

When you don't, He will find someone else to take your place. His overall plan will not be messed up by our rebellion; He looks for those who are willing. Those who are not willing or too slow will miss out on the adventure and on making progress.

Don't miss the moments God has for you. Act. When God makes a promise, we need to be patient and proactive.

Terah stopped halfway. Abraham went all the way and experienced the Promised Land.

God will accomplish His purposes, and He invites us to be part of doing so. When we refuse, others may experience the blessing that we miss.

For example, in Esther 4:14, Mordecai argues that if Esther doesn't step up to save her people, God will still act, but she and her family will be left out of the blessing of being part of the solution.

You only have one life to live, so maximize your life by trusting God every step of the way and in every area of your life. Trust God by living according to the way of Christ! When you do, not only will you be transformed, those you love will be transformed as well.

Just as we need to go to God for guidance in what He wants us to become, we need to go to Him to help us get there.

When God calls you, you can do it. I have seen people use

this process to overcome addictions, work through major issues, breakthrough in areas where they've been stuck for years, or move forward faster toward their God-given destiny.

We need to be ready to declare: I am not going to be a victim to circumstances. With God's help and the help of friends and community, I am going to live out the life He's always wanted me to live. I will take personal responsibility for my future!

A Promise When in Exile

The pandemic of 2020 led to economic devastation for some. It led to illness and death for others. It created an existential crisis leading to more of us struggling with depression and anxiety and anger than ever before.

The pandemic exposed even more the disparity among those who have and those who do not have enough. The pandemic further exposed our tribalism and our nationalism.

According to United Nations chief António Guterres, the pandemic has also brought about a "tsunami of hate and xenophobia, scapegoating and scare-mongering," which he explains gives us the opportunity "to stand up against hate, treat each other with dignity, and take every opportunity to spread kindness."

We are all tempted to fear the future. Some of us feel like we cannot enjoy life until the pandemic ends. Some of us feel like nothing will ever get better. Some of us might remain in denial and just act like everything is okay right now. God is with us in the midst of this. He has not forgotten us. He is still at work in remarkable and amazing ways. And one day God will make all things right. At the same time, God does not promise life won't be hard. The world in which we live is sick and broken, and one day God will make all things right, but that moment is not right now.

There is a beautiful promise in the Scriptures found in Jeremiah 29.

"For I know the plans I have for you," declares the Lord, "plans to prosper you and not to harm you, plans to give you hope and a future." (Jeremiah 29:11, NIV)

Isn't that beautiful?

Like we should for all passages of Scripture, we need to look at the context to fully understand this remarkable promise so we can apply it to our own lives.

Usually, history books are written by the winners, but the Bible is not like that all. Early in the story of God and humanity, we discover that the Hebrew people were "the chosen ones." They were blessed so that through them "all people" would be blessed. They were not blessed for their own sake, but through them all people (other translations say "All nations" or "all families" or "all tribes") will be blessed. God's love is for all people from every tribe, every people group, every nation.

Yet the story of the Bible shows how the chosen people of Israel are enslaved by Egypt for hundreds of years. They were finally free to go into the Promised Land, but they wandered for forty years first. They finally made it to the Promised Land, but it was not just given to them: They had to fight for it. This went on for hundreds of years. Finally, they had a unified kingdom under King David (this was about 3,000 years ago), but this was short-lived. Within just two generations, the kingdom of Israel fell into civil war. Eventually, the Northern kingdom was defeated by the Assyrians, about 700 years before Jesus, and then about 100 years later the Southern kingdom of Judah was defeated by the Babylonians. Many of the people of Israel were taken from their homes and forced to live in Babylon. They were in exile from their home.

Have you been feeling like you have been in exile—apart from the life you wished you still had?

The Scriptures show us how to live with peace, joy, love, and faith even in the wilderness, even when oppressed by others, even amid a system of injustice, even when our home no longer feels like our home, even when we are in exile.

Jeremiah was a messenger of God's justice and grace about 2,600 years ago.

Knowing the context, let's look at the verses surrounding the promise that God knows the plans He has for us and that they are good plans. This passage gives us four ways we can come to understand how to be proactive in this new reality.

Take Care of Your Own and Others

> This is what the Lord Almighty, the God of Israel, says to all those I carried into exile from Jerusalem to Babylon: "Build houses and settle down; plant gardens and eat what they produce. Marry and have sons and daughters; find wives for your sons and give your daughters in marriage, so that they too may have sons and daughters. Increase in number there; do not decrease." (Jeremiah 29:4-6, NIV)

Even in a world that is changing dramatically, we are still responsible to change our world—not the entire planet, but the ones right in front of us.

The passage doesn't stop there. We also see in this passage something remarkable.

> Also, seek the peace and prosperity of the city to which I have carried you into exile. Pray to the Lord for it, because if it prospers, you too will prosper. (Jeremiah 29:7, NIV)

Think about this: In which city did the exiles live? In Babylon! They were living in exile as neighbors of their enemies! And God tells them to seek the good of their city.

This goes against what our culture values or honors. In our culture, we want revenge. Just consider our films, television, music, or watch the news. We burn with a desire for revenge. Seeking the good of our enemies makes no sense!

God's love always extends beyond who we want it to include.

"Seek the peace and prosperity of the city?" What does that even mean? The Hebrew word translated "seek" means to "diligently desire" or even "require." It means more than just hoping for the best; we must do something about it.

We are to "seek" to "diligently desire" or even to "require" "shalom" for where we live.

Shalom is such a big word. It's a word so big that one word in English cannot fully capture the meaning, so the translators used two words: "peace and prosperity." But even that doesn't fully do it justice.

In her book *Roadmap to Reconciliation*, Dr. Brenda Salter McNeil points out that "Shalom" actually refers to "the world as God intended it to be. It's the word most often used in Scripture to describe God's intentions for the world."

We are to work toward the peace, the prosperity, the harmony, the wholeness, the completeness, the welfare, and the tranquility of our city.

- This doesn't just mean we say hello to our neighbors. This means we take care of our neighbors.
- This doesn't just mean we wish our coworkers well. This means we strive to help them succeed.
- This doesn't just mean we hope for the best for those who are struggling in our city with poverty, injustice, inequality, or brokenness. This means we are helping

them overcome their struggles and opening doors of opportunity for them.

Here's the amazing thing: When we do this, our whole city is better, and so are we.

Losing Your Life to Find It

Jesus shares a remarkable spiritual principle:

> "Whoever finds their life will lose it, and whoever loses their life for my sake will find it." (Matthew 10:39, NIV)

One of the positives in this difficult season has been reconnecting with old friends. I received a Facebook message from a woman who had come to faith at Mosaic in Los Angeles while we were there.

It was fifteen years ago that she was spiritually searching, and she came up to me on a Sunday and said: "Sometimes I just wish Jesus was here to give me a hug."

I looked around to see who could give her a hug. Not seeing anyone, I gave her a hug and then it dawned on me.

I told her: "The next time you need a hug, offer one to someone who needs a hug."

You see, every time I have ever hugged someone, they have always hugged me back. Except that one time with my grandpa —but other than that, when you hug someone, they hug you back.

What I did not realize until we started messaging was the backstory. She wrote to me: "I was really struggling because I wanted what those around me had. . . I felt so alone and told you I wanted a hug. I thought that if Jesus were real, and loved me, surely, He'd know I 'needed' to be held and would 'send me' a hug through one of 'His followers.'"

Isn't that amazing? I am so glad I hugged her!

Even more remarkable is what happened after that: McCall decided to follow Jesus.

She wrote me the following: "[Instead of remaining a victim], you helped me see that I was being a volunteer for that loneliness and encouraged me to be an active participant in ALL of my relationships by giving versus 'expecting' to receive. It has been through giving that I get, and God helped teach that to me through you. . . Now whenever I want something, I ask God to help me offer that same thing. And it has worked like a charm for over fifteen years now!"

When you and I seek the good of others, we are blessed.

Laurie Santos, a psychology professor at Yale University, was quoted in an article saying: "The intuition that helping others is the key to our well-being right now fits with science. There's lots of research showing that spending our time and money on other people can often make us happier than spending that same time or money on ourselves."

She also said: "Taking time to do something nice for someone else is a powerful strategy for improving our well-being."

Once again, science proves what the Scriptures have said all along.

Don't Listen to "Fake Religious News"

> Yes, this is what the Lord Almighty, the God of Israel, says: "Do not let the prophets and diviners among you deceive you. Do not listen to the dreams you encourage them to have. They are prophesying lies to you in my name. I have not sent them," declares the Lord. (Jeremiah 29:8-9, NIV)

The people of Israel were ignoring Jeremiah, who was being

honest with them. Instead, they were listening only to those who were telling them what they wanted to hear.

Who are you listening to? Only those who tell you what you want to hear?

Here's the thing. We can find people to affirm whatever we are looking for.

More than anything, we need to listen to God's voice in the midst of all the noise. Too often we get stuck in an echo chamber.

Let me give you an example. When you post an angry or partisan post on Facebook, it makes some of your friends mad, and some of your friends excited, and some of your friends sad that you are so angry and divisive. Before you know it, you have eliminated some of the very people God wants you to love and serve and even influence. They might stop paying attention to you. Also, the Facebook algorithm just sends you the posts of others just like you and hides those with whom you disagree.

Another example comes from the news. We read the news or watch the news on channels or websites that give us what we want to hear. Did you know that news agencies know that the two best ways to generate clicks and viewership is to report on what is most threatening and anxiety producing?

Fake religious news says, "I'm right, I know what's true, so they deserve to be treated this way because God's on my side—the side of truth." It's fake because God says, "Seek the prosperity of your enemies."

"Love your enemies," Jesus said.

We need to avoid fake religious news that pits people against people. Instead, we listen to Jesus, we pray for our enemies, we work for the Shalom of all people in the city by doing what we can to make things right. Above all, not adding to the pitting of people against people, but bringing people together to seek the welfare of all.

When we are filling our minds with bad news, it affects us.

It is important to be informed, but make sure you are taking your thoughts and feelings to God to process, to people in your church family to process, and even to a Christian counselor.

Focus on What Is Most Important

God promises: "For I know the plans I have for you, plans to prosper you and not to harm you, plans to give you hope and a future" (Jeremiah 29:11, NIV).

There is another promise that I am sure may not have been exciting news for those now living in exile.

> This is what the Lord says: "When seventy years are completed for Babylon, I will come to you and fulfill my good promise to bring you back to this place. (Jeremiah 29:10, NIV)

In other words, one day you will get to go back—seventy years from now! That's a long time!

We may not know when the struggle we are facing will end, but we don't have to wait to enjoy life until it is over. We don't need to have any less love, joy, peace, patience, kindness, gentleness, faithfulness, or self-control. The same Spirit of God that gives us the capacity to experience this in the past is just as strong today!

The global pandemic really simplified things for us. For some of us, we recalibrated and stopped doing things during quarantine that we never started back later. For others of us, we started doing things we were not doing before and kept them as part of our lives moving forward.

Jesus summarized the message of the Scriptures with what should be our priorities: loving God and loving people.

When you aren't sure what to do, focus on loving God and on loving people. Just do the next right thing that is in front of you. Keep moving forward, loving God, loving people, and living out what He has called us to do.

A great deal of the Hebrew Scriptures were written during this time of the exile, including the book of Daniel. We can learn to live in exile from the Scriptures. Daniel was one of those taken away from his home and forced to serve in the king's court in Babylon.

At one point, Daniel does something remarkable and selfless. He prays on behalf of his nation in Daniel 9. Even though he was not the cause of their fall, even though he had not been in leadership when the earlier generation made bad decisions that directly affected his life, he prays the following:

> "We have sinned and done wrong. We have been wicked and have rebelled. . . . We are covered with shame. . . . because of our unfaithfulness to you. . . . this disaster has come on us, yet we have not sought the favor of the Lord our God by turning from our sins and giving attention to your truth. . . . We do not make requests of you because we are righteous, but because of your great mercy. Lord, listen! Lord, forgive! Lord, hear and act! For your sake, my God, do not delay, because your city and your people bear your Name." (Daniel 9:4-19, NIV)

We do not have to remain victims of the broken world we inherited from the previous generations. We can ask God for forgiveness and healing. We can ask those hurt by the system set up by previous generations for forgiveness. It's also important that we confess our own failures to stand up for others and confess our own prejudices.

We can work to love people and bring equality and opportunity for people from every nation, every background, every people group. We don't have to be victims of our circumstances. We can rise above and do what God is calling each of us to do.

Dying to Self

Letting go of self is really hard for us because most of us were raised to be independent and free to do what we want when we want. For those of us who grew up in America, this is at the core of what we value. Even our declaration of independence proclaims that it is our God-given right to have "Life, Liberty and the pursuit of Happiness."

Unfortunately, not everyone has had the same opportunities. Even still, it is such a deeply entrenched cultural norm in our country that as Americans we value our freedoms and even make decisions based on what's best for my life, what gives me more liberty, and what will make me happiest.

In direct opposition to this, what we view as heroic are those who give up their rights for the sake of others.

Ultimately, we are so shaped by the story of Jesus that we don't even realize that our superheroes make a sacrifice for the sake others, and against all odds come back from the brink of death. So many films include that narrative! Superheroes like Iron Man in the first Avengers movie, Captain Marvel, Black Panther, and Harry Potter. I am not sure if you agree or not on whether Harry Potter is a superhero, but I do know he has eight movies and an entire theme park about him!

What we know is that heroes give their lives so that others may live, but in the end they survive. It's like they rise from the dead. That's the story of Jesus being retold over and over and over.

So how do we handle these two opposing ideas? I have the right to pursue life, liberty, and happiness, and a hero willingly gives up his or her rights for the rights of others.

Letting go of "self" will help us become the people God created us to be—which, by the way, is also who we all long to become. If you can let go of self, you can become the confident, self-aware, and life-giving person your dog thinks you are rather than struggling with low self-esteem or arrogance and being needy or demanding of others.

So how do we let go of SELF?

By letting go of:

- Selfishness
- Ego
- Labels
- Fear

There are two moments in Jesus' life that will help us, and they both take place during the last week of his life.

Let me give you some context. The last week of Jesus' life was called Passion week. Maybe you've heard of "Passion plays" or the film *Passion of the Christ*.

When we hear the word "passion," we think of love, desire, or enthusiasm, such as when we say something like, "I have a passion for animals or music or film."

We may even exaggerate and say things like we would die for something we are passionate about.

If you look up the word "passion" in Merriam-Webster's Dictionary, it defines passion as "the sufferings of Christ."

You see, God demonstrated who He was passionate about: It's you. Jesus showed how much He loves you by willingly dying on the cross, taking on himself all the evils of humanity.

Before Jesus died on the cross, many Jewish people who heard Him teach and saw Him heal began to think that Jesus must be the Messiah, the promised One who would free His people! They were thinking the Messiah would be their political hero, who would overthrow the Roman government to bring freedom; but Jesus had a bigger agenda. He came to bring life and freedom to people from all nations! He would overthrow the spiritual and religious forces that brought oppression for all people!

On that Palm Sunday, Jesus did not ride into Jerusalem on a horse to bring war. He rode into Jerusalem on a donkey, which was an animal that represented someone coming in peace. As He rode along on the donkey into the city, the people welcomed Jesus with shouts of "Hosanna!" "Blessed is he who comes in the name of the Lord!" "Blessed is the king of Israel!" (John 12:13, NIV).

They were quoting one of the Psalms that predicted the arrival of a Savior. "Hosanna" means "Save us!" or "We're saved!"

Think of how good that must have felt to Jesus!

Have you ever been cheered? Maybe on the soccer field, at a concert where you performed, on a stage after you performed in a play. It's a great feeling to be cheered!

Notice how Jesus responds as the story continues in John 12.

"Now there were some Greeks among those who went up to worship at the festival. They came to Philip. . . . with a request. "Sir," they said, "we would like to see Jesus." Philip got word to Jesus and Jesus replied, "The hour has come for the Son of Man to be glorified." (John 12:20-23, NIV)

At this moment in the story, some of those who were wanting Jesus to overthrow the Roman government were thinking, "Alright! It's time for the Son of Man to be glorified. Jesus is going to show His greatness! Now that the word has gotten out and even the Greeks want to meet the Messiah, this is fantastic! Jesus is more popular than he has ever been!"

But notice what Jesus says next. You see, Jesus sees the Greeks wanting to meet Him as a sign that His time for sacrifice has come.

"I tell you the truth, a grain of wheat must fall to the ground and die to make many seeds. But if it never dies, it remains only a single seed." (John 12:24, NIV)

I'm sure his disciples were thinking: "Jesus, why can't you celebrate your popularity! Why do you have to start talking about death and farming?"

Jesus did not leverage this moment for even more popularity and more power; instead, He predicted He would soon die. He would soon give up everything.

Jesus is pointing out a spiritual principle we intrinsically know: We cannot become the heroes we were created to be unless we are willing to sacrifice for the good of others.

Letting Go of Selfishness

Jesus continues in John 12:

> "Those who love their lives will lose them, but those who hate their lives in this world will keep true life forever." (John 12:25, NIV)

It is so counterintuitive: When we hold onto something too tightly, we break it. When we let go, we get more than we could have ever imagined.

What does it mean to let go of self? Aren't we supposed to take care of ourselves? Doesn't God want us to be happy?

Or you can even get spiritual and ask: Didn't Jesus say to summarize the message of the Scriptures this way?

> "Love the Lord your God with all your heart and with all your soul and with all your mind . . . and to Love your neighbor as yourself." (Matthew 22:37-39, NIV)

How can you let go of self when you are supposed to love your neighbor as you love yourself? And shouldn't we have confidence and high self-esteem?

There is a difference between letting go of self and being

self-aware or being able to take care of yourself. There's a difference between being self-reliant and being selfish or self-centered.

So why should we let go of self?

When we let go of self, we actually have the opportunity to become who we were truly created to be. You see, we were created to love God and love people.

We weren't designed to only take care of ourselves. We were designed for relationship, for creativity, for generating life that lasts.

When we live for self, all that we live for eventually dies, but when we die to self to live for God, God multiplies our lives into the lives of others eternally.

There's a true freedom in letting go and dying to self. I don't have to prove anything or make anything for myself. It's a surrender and trust that my worth is not at all in what I do, but in who I am to God.

The amazing irony of dying to self is that then you're free to fully *be* yourself, try things, risk things, use your gifts, and even *do* more than you ever dreamed, but out of a fullness of *being* who God created you to be.

This full life only comes with God at the center of our lives. The "self" is dethroned from playing ruler of the universe.

Letting Go of Ego

If we are only looking out for ourselves or only looking out for our family, we are missing our purpose in life. Too often pursuing life, liberty, and happiness for ourselves leaves us isolated and unliked by those we stepped on or neglected while striving to get what we wanted.

Instead, we find life, liberty, and something better than happiness, called joy, when we serve others to bring them life, liberty, and happiness. When we make all our decisions only regarding how something affects us—we fail to factor in how our decisions affect other people. We fail to factor in God.

What I think is best for my life and for my family may not actually be good for me or for others. What gives me more freedom from others may not actually be what I truly need to be a healthy person. What I think makes me happiest may not actually be what's ideal in the long run.

The Scriptures talk about this quite a bit but uses words like "pride" and "humility." Take this warning from the book of Proverbs:

"Pride goes before destruction, a haughty spirit before a fall." (Proverbs 16:18, NIV)

If you think too highly of yourself, be careful, or you might be in for a humiliating fall.

Later Peter quotes Proverbs 3:34 when he writes to other followers of Christ who were caught up in the ways of this world.

All of you, clothe yourselves with humility toward one another, because "God opposes the proud but shows favor to the humble." Humble yourselves, therefore, under God's mighty hand, that he may lift you up in due time. Cast all your anxiety on him because he cares for you. (1 Peter 5:5-7, NIV)

It takes humility to take our anxiety to God. Have you found yourself anxious in the midst of the pandemic, the economic uncertainty, the political division, and our racial reckoning?

Worrying is like praying to yourself.

Our minds are working nonstop, as if we can solve all the struggles we face. Instead, humble yourself and take your worries to God. Ask Him for help, guidance, and peace.

God warns us that thinking only about ourselves leads to

pain and destruction. God opposes egotistical pride because of how doing so hurts us and those we love.

What do you call thinking about yourself too highly? Pride or arrogance.

What do you call thinking about yourself too lowly? Having low self-esteem.

The key is to notice in both instances that you are thinking about yourself.

I learned from my friend and mentor Erwin McManus that pride is expressed in these two ways: either thinking too lowly of yourself or too highly of yourself.

We can get stuck thinking so much about ourselves that we miss what God has for us.

That's why God opposes pride, and why He warns us to avoid it!

Why? Because egotistical pride is destructive and insatiable!

Think of the most selfish person you know. Have you ever given him what he wanted, and he remained satisfied? Of course not. Soon he will want more. Because all that the world offers will never fully satisfy an ego-driven person! Not more money. Not more fame. Not more success. Not another woman. Not another family. Nothing in this world will satisfy the human longings that we have.

When you look to yourself and only yourself to meet all your needs, you will be lonely and not live up to your full potential. When you look to others to meet all your needs, you will be hurt and angered.

Remember, we were created to love God and love people, so we need God and others in our lives.

Our culture breeds skepticism. Our past breeds cynicism. As a result, we often reject the very people God has brought to help us. To someone who didn't trust the Church or those in spiritual leadership, I once heard a wise man say, "You cannot say you love Jesus and hate His Bride."

In *Star Trek Into Darkness*, Captain Kirk ends up in a heated argument with his superior. The man who recruited him to serve gets really upset with him and shouts at him: "You don't deserve the chair because you don't respect the chair."

In other words, why should you be given more authority and entrusted with the lives of others when you don't trust the authorities in your life?

Are you really an expert in everything, or are you willing to humble yourself and learn from others who have gotten to where you want to be?

Are you your own spiritual authority, or are you willing to humble yourself to allow others to mentor you and to spend time learning God's message to you in the Scriptures?

Pride limits those to whom we listen and from whom we are willing to learn. When we live with humility, we have access to so much more wisdom!

There is another way besides thinking about yourself.

Humility is the antidote to pride. When we live with humility, we have access to so much more wisdom! We should think of ourselves with humility. Letting go of self means to walk humbly.

"Humility," as we define it, does not actually get to the true meaning of the word in the Scriptures. In English, humility is defined as "a modest or low view of one's own importance." That sounds a lot like thinking too lowly about yourself.

The biblical definition of the word humility is "describing the person who *depends* on the Lord rather than *self*." A humble person has a "a deep sense of one's need for God."

There may be an unhealthy pattern in your life or even an unhealthy relationship because you have been trying to figure it out all on your own. You have been unwilling to ask for help from God or other people.

Letting go of ego means choosing humility instead of pride.

- Are you stuck always thinking about yourself?
- Or are you thinking of others?
- Are you trying to fix your problems on your own?
- Are you considering God's perspective?
- Are you humble enough to ask for help?

Letting Go of Labels

Often life is hard because we don't know who we are, what would satisfy us, or what our purpose might be. So we label ourselves, we label others, and others label us.

I grew up in the 1980s and, yes, it was a lot like *Stranger Things*—although we didn't have to deal with any demogorgons. Those kids are class of 1989. I was class of 1990, and I had the same haircut as Will.

Back in the 1980s, we all had labels. There were the jocks, the preppies, the skaters, and the nerds. Now, I didn't care for those labels, because I felt I didn't really fit in any of them. I was athletic but small, so I played trumpet in the band so I could still go to all the football games without getting hurt. I still loved football, and I got some of the band kids to play football against the choir kids and the kids in drama. We beat both easily. We even played against some of the football players. We got crushed. One of our guys who played French horn got his collarbone broken. It was not a good moment for us. Even still, if I had to have a label, I considered myself a "band jock." I made up my own label!

Here's the problems with labels: They limit us. Rather than letting others label us or affixing a label to ourselves, we need to discover our true identity.

Notice how keenly self-aware Jesus is in this second moment I wanted to share with you. Picking up in the story in John 13, remember Jesus has just told his disciples that his time to give his life has come. Judas had been tempted to betray

Jesus, and then there is this unique description of Jesus. John 13:3 says:

> Jesus knew that the Father had put all things under his power, and that he had come from God and was returning to God. (John 13:3, NIV)

Jesus understood His identity. He knew the power He had. He knew where He was from, and He knew where He was going.

How would you respond if that was you? What do you do when you know who you are, what you are here to do, and where you are going?

- Demonstrate your power?
- Have everyone meet your needs?
- Overthrow the government?
- Make others listen to you?
- Finally get to choose the movie on Disney+?

Instead, Jesus served. He washed the disciples' feet. Look at the very next verse:

> So he got up from the meal, took off his outer clothing, and wrapped a towel around his waist. After that, he poured water into a basin and began to wash his disciples' feet, drying them with the towel that was wrapped around him. (John 13:4-5, NIV)

This is what servants did—not Messiahs, rabbis, prophets, and certainly not the Son of God!

Peter rebuked him: "You're our leader! Leaders don't serve!" Peter refused to let him wash his feet. Jesus gently reminded him he needed to humble himself to receive this, so Peter said, "Then don't just wash my feet, but my whole body!" Jesus reminded him: That's not what I'm offering to do.

Humility is being honest with who you are.

Let me give you something better than a label, let me share with you your true identity.

- You are created in the image of God.
- You are loved by God.
- You need God.
- You have a purpose from God.

God invites you into a relationship with Him. This does not mean reaching some religious milestone. It's not about winning a Bible trivia contest. It's not about doing enough good to outweigh the bad.

It's completely up to you to decide: Do you want a relationship with God? When we let go of trying to find ourselves in our own way and embrace the truth of who we are, it is the path toward true life, genuine liberty, and an eternal happiness. When we say "yes" to following Him, we then seek to do good things out of gratitude and with His help—not to get Him to love us, but because He loves us already!

You can have a faith bigger than your circumstances knowing that God is with you, no matter what is happening all around you and no matter what is happening to you.

To begin that relationship, just say, "Yes, God, I need you. Forgive me. Lead me, Jesus." This really is the same prayer we need to pray every day after that so that we might stay in tune with Him.

Remember, so that we can know Him, God came to us as a person named Jesus. He experienced the limitations of life in a human body on planet earth.

It's difficult for our finite minds to understand how the One God can reveal Himself as Father, Son, and Spirit, but it's because we are stuck in three dimensions, whereas He has no limitations. There is One God, and He has the power to create the Universe, the capacity to dwell among His people as Spirit, and the ability to enter time and space as a human being named Jesus (in Hebrew his name was pronounced "Yeshua," which means "God saves").

God chose to be limited by becoming a human being—born as a helpless infant. He gave up His rights and privilege to become a servant. He chose to humble himself to serve us. He grew up and lived a perfect life, taught with authority, healed those who were sick, created a family for the outcasts, and gained a massive following. Even still, He chose to humble himself to the point where he was betrayed, beaten, falsely accused, stripped, whipped, and humiliated as they mocked him with a crown made of thorns. He chose to humble himself to the point of dying on the cross for the sins of humanity. He entered into death but came out alive on the other side! He rose from the dead proving He was God among us!

This is not just how Jesus died. This is how He lived. He lived with humility, thinking of others rather than Himself.

Dying to self leads to life.

We have to experience a death to the old selfish life so we can be raised back to a new life in Christ as those who follow Him.

You have to have endure the pain of the crucifixion before you can experience the joy of the resurrection.

Notice what Jesus taught his disciples, those who chose to follow Him.

> Then he said to them all: "Whoever wants to be my disciple must deny themselves and take up their cross daily and follow me. For whoever wants to save their life will lose it, but whoever loses their life for me will save it." (Luke 9:23-24, NIV)

I know you may be thinking: "I lose my life serving others all the time, and I am burned out! People are using me!"

That happened to me, but I wasn't serving out of the overflow of my relationship with Jesus. I had let serving others be what filled me up.

Looking for others' praise or approval will never be enough. When we serve others for what it does for us, that is a selfish motive.

Instead, we need to serve out of the overflow of our relationship with God.

Jesus calls us to do what we can only do with His help, so we will depend on Him. Remember: When we say "yes" to following Jesus, we have the same power and authority He has! The same power that rose Jesus from the dead lives in us—the Spirit of God! Jesus reminds us that He has all the authority of God, and we are to go out and make disciples of all nations, and He is with us.

Jesus demonstrated humility, and He invites us to die to self and do the same: to live a life dependent on God, a life loving God and loving others.

Letting Go of Fear

There are times when fear seems rational, such as during the great toilet paper shortage of 2020 at the beginning of the pandemic.

Wherever we may be in this season, whether we chose it or not, we are having to learn to let go. Letting go means asking God for help and asking others for help. It means not trying to fix this on your own or doing things your own way.

Did you know Americans have started praying more? Even those who do not believe began praying more, according to polls taken at the beginning of the global pandemic during quarantine. Twenty-four percent of those who say they do not belong to any religion started praying.

During his time with the disciples, they asked Jesus how to

pray. He taught them a very beautiful prayer that you may have memorized or at least recognize. Don't let the familiarity get in the way of the message of this prayer.

"Our Father in heaven, hallowed be your name, your kingdom come, your will be done, on earth as it is in heaven. Give us today our daily bread. And forgive us our debts, as we also have forgiven our debtors. And lead us not into temptation but deliver us from the evil one." (Matthew 6:9-13, NIV)

This prayer reminds us that God can be our heavenly Father who protects us, provides for us, and forgives us. This prayer reminds us that we are to bring His kingdom to earth as it is in heaven and be the first one to forgive.

But what does "hallowed be your name" mean?

Dr. Carmen Imes explained this in a way that helped this make sense in a new and fresh way for me.

Do you remember the command to not take the Lord's name in vain? Most of us grew up thinking that means you cannot say "God" or "Jesus" like a cuss word. That's why some of us would say things like, "Oh my gosh!" or why my dad would say, "I swan to gosh!" Well, it is that, but it is way more than that.

It's more like this: When we say "yes" to following God, we carry His name. We are His representatives. We can say it like this: "Don't call yourself a Christian, if you aren't going to live like Jesus."

The word "Christian" means "little Christ."

Sadly, the word "Christian" has come to be associated with judgmental, hypocritical, politically-motivated, and angry people.

But that's not who Jesus was and not who we are called to be. We are called to love, to serve, to bring hope, to bring heaven to earth!

If you have been hurt by someone who called himself a

Christian but judged you, I am so sorry. Throughout history, Christians have done more damage to the message of Jesus than anyone else.

At the same time, there have been followers of Jesus who lived like Jesus. Now, they weren't perfect. None of us are. But they loved, served, brought hope, and brought heaven to earth. They "hallowed" the name of God; in other words, they "honored" His name, they glorified His name, they lived up to His name.

These were followers of Jesus who sold their property for those in need, like in Acts 2, or followers of Jesus who served the sick during the plagues in the year 300 in the Roman Empire or in the year 1666 in Europe or in 2019 in China. There were Chinese Christ-followers who are normally oppressed for their faith that served during the height of the coronavirus in Wuhan. They were able to serve and tell people about the love of Jesus because they were wearing masks and surveillance cameras were unable to recognize them.

Why would they do that? Because followers of Jesus know that this life is not all there is. We are promised a life in God's presence for all eternity. That's what heaven is! We are citizens of heaven who are bringing heaven to earth with God's help and out of gratitude for all God has done for us!

What's after this life gives us hope. Bringing heaven to earth gives us purpose.

When we let go of self and allow God to lead us, we become who He created us to be!

We experience the blessing of a life connected to God, and that blessing impacts those we love.

Reflection:

What do you know you should do in your life right now that you are refusing to do or putting off until later?

How can you take more personal responsibility for your future?

When have you experienced the joy of how serving others brings us life?

In this season, who are the people God wants you to love, serve, and even influence towards following Jesus?

Are you willing to ask God for help, forgiveness, and guidance on how to move forward, no matter what you may be facing?

Work through the section on "Sacrifices" in Appendix A.

APPENDIX A: A PROCESS TO
CREATE A BETTER FUTURE

WHAT DOES GOD WANT FOR YOUR FUTURE?
HOW CAN YOU GET THERE?

THE PROCESS:

WORK through the questions on God's Calling before going through the sections on Becoming Receptive, Becoming Tenacious, Becoming Intentional, and Becoming Proactive. Consider working through these questions in this book or in a journal.

In what areas are you currently serving out of passion?
In what areas are you currently serving out of obligation? If you were passionate about this area in the past, what changed in you or the situation?

How do your preferences shape what may be your calling?

How do your strengths shape what may be your calling?

How do your underlying motivations shape what may be your calling?

When in your life have you felt most alive?
Consider Psalm 37:4, which says: "When we delight ourselves in God, He gives us the desires of our heart."

With this being the case, when you were closest to God, what were you wanting to do with your life?

In what areas of your life have you been affirmed for your efforts?

In what ways do you like to serve others?

Do you have personal core values?
If so, what are they?

If not, consider Michael Warden's definition of a value and come up with your top five. "A value is any context, quality or way of engaging with life that fills you up, gets your blood going, and nourishes your soul. Essentially, a value can be anything that makes your heart come alive."

Do you have a personal mission statement?
If so, evaluate on a scale from 0 to 10 how well you are doing at living out this statement?

If not, what do you think would be elements you could include in one?

How has God spoken to you through the Scriptures, through your church family, or through that "still, small voice" about your purpose?

What are areas of need you see around you that you sense need to be met?

What does God want you to do for the world?

This is different from what we want God to do for us. Give him all of your desires and ask Him to give back to you what is His best.

We can tell God is speaking when a thought that comes to mind is selfless, takes courage, and is consistent with His character. Considering this, what do you sense God is calling you to do?

BECOMING RECEPTIVE

WHAT IS GOD CALLING YOU TO DO?

(Big Picture and Next Steps)
Examples of Big Picture types of callings:

- To become a doctor, a pastor, an entrepreneur, etc.
- To get married
- To have a healthy marriage
- To become a healthy person
- To become a parent
- To overcome an addiction

Examples of Next Steps types of callings (Next Steps are specific and short-term, but also part of the Big Picture calling God has for your life):

- Complete a particular project
- Heal a particular relationship
- Go through the Twelve Steps
- Lose twenty pounds

Write down some of the things that you sense God is calling you toward:

Do you see a theme?
Choose one Big Picture calling or one Next Steps calling and then answer the following in light of that particular calling.

BECOMING TENACIOUS

WHAT TRIALS HAVE KEPT YOU FROM YOUR CALLING?

(Events, People, Fears, etc.)
Write down the things that have happened to you that have
slowed you down from your calling:

BECOMING INTENTIONAL

WHAT TEMPTATIONS HAVE KEPT YOU FROM YOUR CALLING?

(Struggles, Generational Sins, etc.)
Write down the things that you have done that have derailed you or distracted you from your calling:

BECOMING PROACTIVE

WHAT SACRIFICES DO YOU NEED TO MAKE TO LIVE OUT YOUR CALLING?

Consider the following:

- Some of us lack the courage to do something new. Some of us lack the character to stay and work on improving what we have.
- Stop overcommitting. Being committed to many things means you aren't really committed to anything.
- If you aren't taking care of yourself now, you won't be able to take care of others later.

Write down what you need to stop doing or start doing to make progress:

Choose one or two others to keep you accountable with these new behaviors. Ideally one person should be modeling for you what you want to become and the type of person you want to become, and the other person is someone who needs your help in making progress in their own life.

APPENDIX B: A PERSPECTIVE TO MAKE PROGRESS

I have been crucified with Christ and I no longer live, but Christ lives in me. The life I now live in the body, I live by faith in the Son of God, who *loved me and ^gave himself for me. (Galatians 2:20)

What helps us move forward:

- Remember Whose you are and for Whom you live
- Remember all He's done for you—let gratitude motivate your progress

Consider: in what ways has God loved you and given to you in such a way that helps you become who He created you to be?

*How has God shown His love for you today? This past week? This past year? Across the course of your life?

^How has God provided for you today? This past week? This past year? Across the course of your life?

"His divine power has given us everything we need for a godly life through our knowledge of him who called us by his own glory and goodness." (2 Peter 1:3)

APPENDIX C: THE FRUITFUL LIFE OVERVIEW

WHAT DOES GOD WANT FOR YOUR FUTURE?

HOW CAN YOU GET THERE?
AN EVALUATION:

THROUGH UNLOCKING an ancient truth revealed by Jesus Christ, we can experience a life beyond our imagination and beyond our limitations. In his lifetime, Jesus revealed for the first time an ancient truth that prophets and the righteous had longed to discover. The secret had been hidden for ages. Jesus revealed a new way of looking at life, a new way of organizing the future. God's design for our lives is that we would be productive, generative, and creative.

Start with an understanding of who you are and where you are now.

Which soil are you?

"A farmer went out to sow his seed. As he was scattering the seed, some fell along the path, and the birds came and ate it up. Some fell on rocky places, where it did not have much soil. It sprang up quickly, because the soil was shallow. But when the sun came up, the plants were scorched, and they withered because they had no root. Other seed fell among thorns, which grew up and choked the plants. Still other seed fell on good soil, where it produced a crop—a hundred, sixty or thirty times what was sown. Whoever has ears, let them hear."

The disciples came to him and asked, "Why do you speak to the people in parables?"

He replied, "Because the knowledge of the secrets of the kingdom of heaven has been given to you, but not to them. Whoever has will be given more, and they will have an abundance. Whoever does not have, even what they have will be taken from them. This is why I speak to them in parables:

"Though seeing, they do not see; though hearing, they do not hear or understand. In them is fulfilled the prophecy of Isaiah:

"'You will be ever hearing but never understanding; you will be ever seeing but never perceiving. For this people's heart has become calloused; they hardly hear with their ears, and they have closed their eyes. Otherwise they might see with their eyes, hear with their ears, understand with their hearts and turn, and I would heal them.'

But blessed are your eyes because they see, and your ears because they hear. For truly I tell you, many prophets and righteous people longed to see what you see but did not see it, and to hear what you hear but did not hear it. "Listen then to what the parable of the sower means:

When anyone hears the message about the kingdom and does not understand it, the evil one comes and snatches away what was sown in their heart. This is the seed sown along the path. The seed falling on rocky ground refers to someone who hears the word and at once receives it with joy. But since they have no root, they last only a short time. When trouble or persecution comes because of the word, they quickly fall away. The seed falling among the thorns refers to someone who hears the word, but the worries of this life and the deceitfulness of wealth choke the word, making it unfruitful. But the seed falling on good soil refers to someone who hears the word and understands it. This is the one who produces a crop, yielding a hundred, sixty or thirty times what was sown." (Matthew 13:8-23)

- Some of us have a hardened heart. We have been walked on. We haven't heard from God in a long time. We don't want to hear from God.
- Some of us have a shallow faith. Our faith is based entirely on our circumstances and how we feel at the time.
- Some of us have been distracted by temptations we keep falling into over and over.
- Some of us are in a good place. We are seeing change in our lives and change in the ones we care about, and it's happening through us!
- Some of us see a glimpse of more than one. We are seeing God do good things or even great things, and we are on the edge of falling back into darkness.

Wherever you are, Jesus pointed us toward becoming fruitful which means transformed by God and helping others transform.

In the parable of the sower, Jesus shared how we can become who He intends for us to be. We can become like the good soil that bears tremendous fruit (Matthew 13:1-23, Mark 4:1-20, and John 8:4-15).

Jesus' parable points out that we struggle to become who we were created to be when we fail in any of the following areas: hearing God's voice, overcoming the trials we face, overcoming the temptations that distract us, or not doing what we hear from the Lord. To avoid these pitfalls, we can discover our God-given destinies by becoming receptive, tenacious, intentional, and proactive.

Becoming Receptive

At times we fail to experience the fullness of life because we lack receptivity. Rather than remaining hardened to spiritual things, we can become vulnerable. This vulnerability or openness enables us to hear God's voice and discern His destinies for our lives.

Becoming Tenacious

When challenges or difficulties arise, too often we give up on our spiritual journey. Instead, we need to take the time to develop a deeper faith which involves gaining a broader perspective to overcome the trials in our lives.

Becoming Intentional

The world is filled with internal and external distractions. Our lives become thorny, complicated, and overwhelming. Rather than succumb to the stress and pressures, we can simplify our lives and find clarity. By becoming intentional, we can overcome temptations that have kept us from experiencing the full lives offered to us in Christ.

Becoming Proactive

The natural result of following Christ is a life described as fruitful, rich, and productive. If we can become receptive, tenacious, and intentional, we will find ourselves in a position to experience our destiny. Knowing our calling is a tremendous challenge. Choosing to act on our calling is sometimes even tougher. We can learn to be more responsive to God.

Determining which soil best describes where we are now helps us make the adjustments necessary to become people of expansive influence—transformed and transforming others.

We can help move someone out of isolation (Hardened, Shallow, Distracted, and Desolate) and beyond independence (Vulnerable, Deep, Clear, and Creative) to become a person of expansive influence (Prophet, Guide, Trailblazer, and Catalyst). Most people feel that independence is the right goal, but in God's design for our lives, He created us to live lives of influence.

	ISOLATION	INDEPENDENCE	INFLUENCE
SOIL #1 Receptive	Hardened	Vulnerable	Prophet
SOIL #2 Tenacious	Shallow	Deep	Guide
SOIL #3 Intentional	Distracted	Clear	Trailblazer
SOIL #4 Proactive	Desolate	Creative	Catalyst

APPENDIX D: THE FRUITFUL LIFE ASSESSMENT

After answering a series of questions, you will be able to determine the areas in your life that are needing growth, as well as the areas in which you are strong. This process helps you determine the best path toward influencing others—whether you more naturally influence others as a prophet, guide, trailblazer, or catalyst.

Please rate each of the following questions on a scale of 1 to 5 using the descriptions below:

1 = Not at all true of me
2 = Very seldom true of me
3 = Occasionally true of me
4 = Often true of me
5 = Always true of me

Write down the number corresponding to the description that best describes you for each of the following questions:

1. _____ I spend time reading the Bible each day.

2. _____ I keep commitments I have made, no matter what.

3. _____ I do not easily fall into temptation.

4. _____ I forgive others quickly.

5. _____ I know when God is speaking to me.

6. _____ I overcome trials easily.

7. _____ I am not easily persuaded by peer pressure.

8. _____ I seek out relationships with others who will keep me accountable.

9. _____ I want to hear God's voice each day.

10. _____ People would consider me as optimistic rather than pessimistic.

11. _____ When I am tempted in various ways, I quote Scripture and pray.

12. _____ I do what I know I am supposed to do at home, at work, and/or at school.

13. _____ I seek out others who know God personally for advice.

14. _____ I have a high tolerance for pain and suffering.

15. _____ I rarely struggle with bad habits.

16. _____ I do not do what I am not supposed to do at home, at work, and/or at school.

17. _____ I go to God first when I need guidance.

18. _____ I enjoy discovering the ways others have overcome their struggles.

19. _____ In my thought life, I am able to distinguish between my thoughts, temptations from Satan, and guidance from God.

20. _____ "Not my will but Yours be done" is my constant prayer to God.

21. _____ I do not mind a gentle rebuke from someone in my life.

22. _____ I bounce back quickly after failing.

23. _____ My lifestyle matches my beliefs.

24. _____ When I know what God desires for me to do, I immediately do it.

25. _____ I tell other people what God is telling me.

26. _____ I look to help others overcome their difficult situations.

27. _____ I am able to offer solutions to others for a way out of their bad patterns.

28. _____ I share about my relationship with Jesus Christ with others who do not yet believe in Him.

29. _____ I help other people discover God's guidance for their lives.

30. _____ People come to me for help in overcoming their trials.

31. _____ I have helped others overcome temptations.

32. _____ I am willing to confront another person who is making a mistake.

33. _____ I encourage people I do not know.

34. _____ People come to me for comfort in the midst of their trials.

35. _____ I enjoy talking to people about their personal struggles.

36. _____ I seek out relationships with others who want to be kept accountable.

37. _____ People approach me for spiritual advice.

38. _____ I help others see the good in the midst of a bad situation.

39. _____ When I sin, I approach others for help.

40. _____ I bring others along with me while I am serving God.

Scoring Your Assessment

The numbers below correspond to the numbers of each question in The Fruitful Life Assessment. Write down your response to each of the assessment questions (1, 2, 3, 4, or 5) in the corresponding box. Once you have finished writing down your scores, add each column up and write down your totals.

PROPHET	GUIDE	TRAILBLAZER	CATALYST
1	2	3	4
5	6	7	8
9	10	11	12
13	14	15	16
17	18	19	20
21	22	23	24
TOTAL A	TOTAL A	TOTAL A	TOTAL A

PROPHET	GUIDE	TRAILBLAZER	CATALYST
25	26	27	28
29	30	31	32
33	34	35	36
37	38	39	40
TOTAL B	TOTAL B	TOTAL B	TOTAL B

TOTAL A	TOTAL A	TOTAL A	TOTAL A
TOTAL B	TOTAL B	TOTAL B	TOTAL B
PROPHET GRAND TOTAL	GUIDE GRAND TOTAL	TRAILBLAZER GRAND TOTAL	CATALYST GRAND TOTAL

Results #1 – The Fruitful Life Skills Ranking

Rank the grand totals from the columns (prophet, guide, trailblazer, and catalyst) in order from highest to lowest.

<u>Column Name and Score</u>

1st—

2nd—

3rd—

4th—

This first ranking indicates your natural preference for influencing others. All four of these skills are necessary for the greatest impact in influencing others spiritually. Your high score indicates the skill with which you have the greatest potential for effectiveness. When you are going in the right direction in your life, you will influence others more effectively in this highest area. Your lowest score indicates the skill which needs the greatest effort for improvement. Your low score(s) indicates the area keeping you from greater spiritual influence in the lives of your family, neighbors, coworkers, and friends.

Notice the following descriptions for each of these skills:

Prophet – able to hear God's voice and helps others do the same
Guide – able to overcome trials and helps others do the same
Trailblazer – able to overcome temptations and helps others do the same
Catalyst – able to obey God and helps others do the same

Results #2 – Spiritual Independence Continuums

Receptivity Scale

What was "Total A" in the "Prophet" column?
Mark your spot on the Receptivity Scale below:

SPIRITUALLY HARDENED	SELDOM VULNERABLE	OCCASIONALLY VULNERABLE	OFTEN VULNERABLE	ALWAYS VULNERABLE
6	12	18	24	30

This scale answers the question, "How spiritually receptive am I?"

Tenacity Scale

What was "Total A" in the "Guide" column?
Mark your spot on the Tenacity Scale below:

SPIRITUALLY SHALLOW	SELDOM DEEP	OCCASIONALLY DEEP	OFTEN DEEP	ALWAYS DEEP
6	12	18	24	30

This scale answers the question, "How tenacious am I?"

Intentionality Scale

What was "Total A" in the "Trailblazer" column?
Mark your spot on the Intentionality Scale below:

SPIRITUALLY THORNY	SELDOM CLEAR	OCCASIONALLY CLEAR	OFTEN CLEAR	ALWAYS CLEAR
6	12	18	24	30

This scale answers the question, "How spiritually distracted am I?"

Proactivity Scale

What was "Total A" in the "Catalyst" column?
Mark your spot on the Proactivity Scale below:

SPIRITUALLY DESOLATE	SELDOM FRUITFUL	OCCASIONALLY FRUITFUL	OFTEN FRUITFUL	ALWAYS FRUITFUL
6	12	18	24	30

This scale answers the question, "How spiritually responsive am I?"

Results #3 – Influence Continuum

Prophet Scale

What was "Total B" in the "Prophet" column?
Mark your spot on the Prophet Scale below:

NOT PROPHETIC	SELDOM PROPHETIC	OCCASIONALLY PROPHETIC	OFTEN PROPHETIC	ALWAYS PROPHETIC
←				→
4	8	12	16	20

This scale answers the question, "How often do I help others hear from God?"

Guide Scale

What was "Total B" in the "Guide" column?
Mark your spot on the Guide Scale below:

NOT GUIDE	SELDOM GUIDE	OCCASIONALLY GUIDE	OFTEN GUIDE	ALWAYS GUIDE
←				→
4	8	12	16	20

This scale answers the question, "How often do I help others overcome trials?"

Trailblazer Scale

What was "Total B" in the "Trailblazer" column?
Mark your spot on the Trailblazer Scale below:

NOT TRAILBLAZER	SELDOM TRAILBLAZER	OCCASIONALLY TRAILBLAZER	OFTEN TRAILBLAZER	ALWAYS TRAILBLAZER
←				→
4	8	12	16	20

This scale answers the question, "How often do I help others overcome temptation?"

Catalyst Scale

What was "Total B" in the "Lifegiver" column?
Mark your spot on the Lifegiver Scale below:

NOT CATALYST	SELDOM CATALYST	OCCASIONALLY CATALYST	OFTEN CATALYST	ALWAYS CATALYST
4	8	12	16	20

This scale answers the question, "How often do I help others obey God?"

A Description of the Types of Influencers

Prophets hear from God and share with others what they have heard. They desire to hear God's voice and help others learn to do the same. They overcome spiritual silence by distinguishing God's voice from among the crowd. Prophets choose to become God's messengers of hope.

Guides, like Sherpas, climb mountains others would never dare to attempt or never think they could. Trials and challenges do not keep them from continuing their journey. Guides develop a high tolerance for suffering and help others overcome their struggles as well.

Trailblazers have learned to overcome temptations personally as well as how to help others do the same. They help focus others in the right direction.

Catalysts overcome rebellion and desolation to become

generative and creative. The result of their efforts with others is exponentially more effective than attempting to serve God on their own. They recognize the importance of bringing others with them on the journey.

APPENDIX E: RESOURCES

- www.ericbryant.org
- *Not Like Me: Learning to Love, Serve, and Influence a Divided World*
- Catalyzing Community: a non-profit organization that exists to help churches, non-profit organizations, and businesses find their calling, catalyze community, and create change agents. More at www. ericbryant.org.
- *The Post-Christian Podcast* reframes, simplifies, and focuses on our mission to make disciples in a post Christian culture. We discuss reaching new people and raising up leaders while removing the barriers of churchianity. Subscribe and rate wherever you listen to podcasts.
- Books by Erwin McManus, John Burke, Dan Kimball, Tim Keller, Margaret Feinberg, John Mark Comer, Brenda Salter McNeil, N.T. Wright, and Derwin Gray

ENDNOTES

Becoming Receptive: Overcoming a Hard Heart

Plato.Stanford.edu. (2020, November 21). "Aristotle's Metaphysics."

Peterson, Eugene. (2002). *The Message: The Bible in Contemporary Language.* Colorado Springs, CO: NavPress.

StarTribune.com *(2013, August 15).* "New mammal species discovered: a raccoon-sized critter with teddy bear looks."

BBC.com (2013, August 15). "Olinguito: 'Overlooked' mammal carnivore is major discovery."

Klavan, Andrew. (2016). *The Great Good Thing: A Secular Jew Comes to Faith in Christ.* Nashville, TN: Thomas Nelson.

Keller, Timothy. (2016). *Prayer: Experiencing Awe and Intimacy with God.* New York: NY. Penguin Books.

Comer, John Mark. (2017). *God Has A Name*. Grand Rapids, MI: Zondervan.

Friesen, Garry and J. Robin Maxon. (2004). *Decision-Making and the Will of God: A Biblical Alternative to the Traditional View*. Portland, OR: Multnomah.

Bowling for Soup, "(Ohio) Come Back to Texas," track 5 on *A Hangover You Don't Deserve*, Jive Records, 2004, compact disc.

Becoming Tenacious: Overcoming Trials

BBCAmerica.com. (2015, April 9). "50 Sir Winston Churchill Quotes To Live By."

Burke, John. (2014). *Unshockable Love: How Jesus Changes the World Through Imperfect People*. Grand Rapids, MI: Baker Books.

Friends in Recovery. (1994). *The Twelve Steps: A Spiritual Journey (Tools for Recovery)*. Boise, ID: RPI Publications.

Walley, Dean. (1967). *So Many Kinds of Love*. Kansas City, MO: Hallmark Publishing.

Kahneman, Daniel. (2013). *Thinking Fast and Slow*. New York, NY: Farrar, Straus and Giroux.

Tim Mackie, "Lamentations," Bible Project video, 7:17, June 30, 2016, https://bibleproject.com/explore/video/lamentations/.

Barker, Kenneth L. (editor). (2011). *NIV Study Bible*. Grand Rapids, MI: Zondervan.

Wright, N.T. (2011). *New Testament for Everyone: Complete Eighteen-Volume Set*. Louisville, KY: Westminster John Knox Press.

Kimball, Dan. (2020). *How (Not) to Read the Bible: Making Sense of the Anti-Women, Anti-Science, Pro-Violence, Pro-Slavery and Other Crazy-Sounding Parts of Scripture*. Grand Rapids, MI: Zondervan.

Frankl, Viktor. (2006). *Man's Search for Meaning*. Boston, MA: Beacon Press.

Becoming Intentional: Overcoming Temptations

Dweck, Carol. (2007). *Mindset: The New Psychology of Success*. New York, NY: Ballatine Books.

Burke, John. (2007). *No Perfect People Allowed: Creating a Come-as-you-are Culture in the Church*. Grand Rapids, MI: Zondervan.

Seligman, Martin. (2006). *Learned Optimism: How to Change Your Mind and Your Life*. New York, NY: Knopf Doubleday Publishing Group.

Ecclesia Bible Society (editor). (2012). *The Voice Bible: Step Into the Story of Scripture*. Nashville, TN: Thomas Nelson.

NPR.com. (2020, January 23). "Most Americans Are Lonely, And Our Workplace Culture May Not Be Helping."

Cigna.com. (2018, May 18). "New Cigna Study Reveals Loneliness at Epidemic Levels in America."

Housman, Jeff and Steve Dorman (2005). "The Alameda County

Study: A Systematic, Chronological Review" (PDF). *American Journal of Health Education.*

TheAtlantic.com. (2012, May). "Is Facebook Making Us Lonely?"

McManus, Erwin. (2010). *Uprising: A Revolution of the Soul.* Nashville, TN: Thomas Nelson.

Becoming Proactive: Overcoming Selfishness

Chapman, Gary. (2015). *The 5 Love Languages: The Secret to Love that Lasts.* Chicago: IL. Northfield Publishing.

UN.org. (2020, May 8). "Secretary-General Denounces 'Tsunami' of Xenophobia Unleashed amid COVID-19, Calling for All-Out Effort against Hate Speech."

Salter McNeil, Brenda. (2015). *Roadmap to Reconciliation: Moving Communities into Unity, Wholeness and Justice.* Downers Grove, IL: InterVarsity Press.

NBCNewYork.com. (2020, May 22). "In Coronavirus Chaos, Some Find Solace, Purpose in Helping Others."

ABOUT THE AUTHOR

Dr. Eric Michael Bryant serves with Gateway Church in Austin as an Executive Pastor, South Austin Campus Pastor, and as part of the teaching team along with Senior Pastor John Burke. Gateway is known for their mottos: "no perfect people allowed" and "come as you are, but don't stay that way."

From 1998-2010, Eric served as part of the leadership team with Erwin McManus at Mosaic in Los Angeles, a church known for its creativity and diversity. The four years prior to that he helped plant a church in Seattle, WA.

Eric earned his doctorate in Entrepreneurial Leadership at Bethel Seminary in St. Paul, MN.

Eric is the author of *Not Like Me: Loving, Serving, and Influencing Our Divided World*, host of The Post-Christian Podcast, and content provider at www.ericbryant.org.

Eric lives with his wife, Deborah in South Austin.

facebook.com/ericmichaelbryant

twitter.com/ericbryant

instagram.com/ericbryant

ALSO BY ERIC MICHAEL BRYANT

Now more than ever is the time for us to discover how to create genuine unity among people from a variety of backgrounds and worldviews.

Not Like Me urges readers—women and men, democrats and republicans, church leaders and lay people from every background—to create a new future that connects God's heart by removing the religious baggage of Christianity to discover the world Jesus intended.

- The Church can be an example of loving and diverse community.

- The Church can bring healing and unity.
- The Church can reach those too often overlooked, ignored, or misunderstood.
- The Church can overcome our negative stereotype.

Through stories and insights gleaned from Eric's own personal experiences and failures, the experiences of others, and the life and teachings of Jesus, readers will discover how to move beyond ethnic, racial, cultural, and ideological barriers toward genuine friendship with others that can lead to personal and community transformation.

The 10th anniversary edition of *Not Like Me* inspires and equips us to develop diverse communities, resolve conflict, overcome bitterness, create a better future, and even heal our fractured world.

To purchase *Not Like Me* or *Fruitful* in bulk for small groups or a sermon series, contact eric@ericbryant.org for a deeply discounted rate.